Distinguished Teachers on Effective Teaching

*Observations on Teaching by College
Professors Recognized by the Council for
Advancement and Support of Education*

Peter G. Beidler, *Editor*
Lehigh University

NEW DIRECTIONS FOR TEACHING AND LEARNING

KENNETH E. EBLE, *Editor-in-Chief*
University of Utah, Salt Lake City

Number 28, Winter 1986

Paperback sourcebooks in
The Jossey-Bass Higher Education Series

Jossey-Bass Inc., Publishers
San Francisco • London

Peter G. Beidler (ed.).
Distinguished Teachers on Effective Teaching.
New Directions for Teaching and Learning, no. 28.
San Francisco: Jossey-Bass, 1986.

New Directions for Teaching and Learning
Kenneth E. Eble, *Editor-in-Chief*

New Directions for Teaching and Learning is published quarterly
by Jossey-Bass Inc., Publishers. Second class postage paid at
San Francisco, California, and at additional mailing offices.
POSTMASTER: Send address changes to Jossey-Bass Inc., Publishers,
433 California Street, San Francisco, California 94104.

Editorial correspondence should be sent to the Editor-in-Chief,
Kenneth E. Eble, Department of English, University of Utah,
Salt Lake City, Utah 84112.

Library of Congress Catalog Card Number 85-81906

International Standard Serial Number ISSN 0271-0633

International Standard Book Number ISBN 1-55542-995-5

Cover art by WILLI BAUM

Manufactured in the United States of America

Ordering Information

The paperback sourcebooks listed below are published quarterly and can be ordered either by subscription or single-copy.

Subscriptions cost $40.00 per year for institutions, agencies, and libraries. Individuals can subscribe at the special rate of $30.00 per year *if payment is by personal check.* (Note that the full rate of $40.00 applies if payment is by institutional check, even if the subscription is designated for an individual.) Standing orders are accepted.

Single copies are available at $9.95 when payment accompanies order, and *all single-copy orders under $25.00 must include payment.* (California, New Jersey, New York, and Washington, D.C., residents please include appropriate sales tax.) For billed orders, cost per copy is $9.95 plus postage and handling. (Prices subject to change without notice.)

Bulk orders (ten or more copies) of any individual sourcebook are available at the following discounted prices: 10–49 copies, $8.95 each; 50–100 copies, $7.96 each; over 100 copies, *inquire.* Sales tax and postage and handling charges apply as for single copy orders.

Please note that these prices are for the academic year 1986–1987 and are subject to change without prior notice. Also, some titles may be out of print and therefore not available for sale.

To ensure correct and prompt delivery, all orders must give either the *name of an individual* or an *official purchase order number.* Please submit your order as follows:

Subscriptions: specify series and year subscription is to begin.
Single Copies: specify sourcebook code (such as, TL1) and first two words of title.

Mail orders for United States and Possessions, Latin America, Canada, Japan, Australia, and New Zealand to:
Jossey-Bass Inc., Publishers
433 California Street
San Francisco, California 94104

Mail orders for all other parts of the world to:
Jossey-Bass Limited
28 Banner Street
London EC1Y 8QE

New Directions for Teaching and Learning Series
Kenneth E. Eble, *Editor-in-Chief*

Contents

Do college professors feel good about their jobs, or would they secretly rather be doing something else?

Editor's Notes

In 1981 the Council for Advancement and Support of Education (CASE) initiated its annual Professor of the Year selection. That year, and every year since, colleges and universities around the nation made nominations from among the ranks of their faculty. And that year, and every year since, a selection panel has read the letters of nomination and support and made a selection of a winner and several finalists. At this writing, there have been more than twenty finalists and, selected from among those, five award winners. Those finalists are among the most distinguished professors in the nation. Not only singled out for nomination by their own institutions, they were also chosen from among many other nominees from many other colleges and universities. Although there is always an element of the arbitrary and an element of good fortune in any such selection process, few would doubt that these CASE Professor of the Year finalists constitute a group worth hearing from on the subject of teaching.

Teaching and learning are complex and important subjects and it is troubling that the world rarely asks good teachers about them. This sourcebook is designed to give some good teachers a chance to say something about important subjects they know and care about: college teaching and the way students learn. This sourcebook is about that special power loving teachers have—the power to touch.

When I began work on this volume, I first decided to see whether these award-winning professors would agree to answer a series of questions about their views on teaching and the profession of teaching. Most of them agreed to do so, and I soon had a set of questions in the mail to them. The questions ranged widely: What professor most influenced you? What is the relationship between your teaching and the "real world" beyond the classroom? What is the connection between the teaching you do and the research you do? How do students learn? If the questions were diverse, the answers from this varied, independent, and articulate group of professors were even more diverse.

In the pages that follow, I have selected eight of these questions and built a chapter around each. I begin each chapter with a discussion of my own views on the topic and a brief explanation of why I asked the question, and then I finish the chapter with selections from the answers of the other CASE finalists. I have condensed most of the written answers I received and have made minor stylistic alterations to several of them. I have made no attempt to "force" a unanimity of views where none was apparent, although I have tried to group similar responses together.

1

Information on each of the participating CASE finalists appears in the first chapter.

I am grateful to the Council for Advancement and Support of Education for attempting to identify and recognize good college teachers, to Marion Egge and James Wallace for editorial assistance, to Ken Eble for his encouragement of this somewhat unusual approach to a volume in his series, and especially to my fellow CASE finalists for responding to my questions with such candor, completeness, and good spirit.

Peter G. Beidler
Editor

Peter G. Beidler is Lucy G. Moses Professor of English at Lehigh University. He was named CASE Professor of the Year in 1983.

Somewhere behind almost every good professor is another good professor, a man or a woman who, probably without trying, showed someone who had no notion of following a career in teaching that this was the good—or at least the right—life.

"He Changed My Life": CASE Professors and Those Who Influenced Them

Teaching is a "people" activity. We professors teach a subject, to be sure, but we are not professors without the people we teach it to, and we would not have become professors without the people we learned it from.

Tacky House and Wilted Clothes

When I was an undergraduate, the one thing I was sure of was that I did not want to be a teacher. Teaching was too sedentary. It meant a small tacky house and wilted clothes and a rusty car and then doing the same thing year after boring year. Teachers did not make money. Nor did teachers make love; they merely read about it. Being a teacher was all books and ideas. I wanted a life of things and adventures and love.

At Earlham College in 1962, I drew Wayne Booth for freshman English. He had a tacky house four blocks from campus. He wore wilted clothes. He owned no car, not even a rusty one. He made us read novels and poetry about love. He was all books and ideas. But the way Wayne Booth taught English, it did not seem like a sedentary subject. He made it seem important for us to know how to write. He made adventures out of books. He found a way to let us freshmen know that ideas were not just ideas. They changed

P. G. Beidler (ed.). *Distinguished Teachers on Effective Teaching.*
New Directions for Teaching and Learning, no. 28. San Francisco: Jossey-Bass, Winter 1986.

people and nations and worlds. And as for love, Wayne Booth found a way to let us know that he could have written that book.

Wayne Booth had a way of letting students, even freshmen, walk into his life.

I did not walk out of my last class with Wayne Booth wanting to be a teacher, but already, at the end of my freshman year, I felt a shift in my interests. My interest in a math major waned as the fun of solving number problems melted away in the face of the abstract theoretical stuff that seemed, somewhere in the second semester of calculus, to have replaced it. My interest in geology waned when I realized that rocks could never know love and that those dinosaurs who had left their bones and footprints in the primordial slime had never known the excitement of having an idea. It did not occur to me then to become a teacher, but when I found myself signing up for a major in English halfway through my sophomore year, I realized that I was doing so because Wayne Booth had touched me. I vaguely remember thinking that touching people was perhaps not such a bad thing to do with one's life . . . if one was a Wayne Booth.

I was not a Wayne Booth. I am still not a Wayne Booth. But Wayne Booth showed me that there was adventure in the world of ideas. He let me know that love was not something to snicker at. He showed me that wearing wilted clothes and driving no car was quite all right, because those things did not matter. Having been taught all those things, of course, I was perhaps inevitably destined to become a teacher. In ways that neither he nor I knew at the time, Wayne Booth had made me a different person, had shown me that teachers have the power to touch human lives.

When I began to write the questions for the CASE finalists to answer, I knew that one of these questions would have to be about the most influential teachers they had known. I knew that I could not say much about teaching without thinking first about Wayne Booth, if only to get myself in the proper mood. I wanted the other CASE finalists to get in the proper mood, as well. My first question, then, was:

Name and describe the teacher who most influenced you in your years as a college undergraduate. What was special about him or her? (We have all had several fine teachers, of course, but I do not want this question to turn into a series of public "thank you's" to all of your former good teachers. For this question, please try to isolate the most special . . . one.)

In the rest of this chapter, I shall briefly introduce in alphabetical order each of the CASE finalists who agreed to send me answers to this and the other questions. This chapter, then, will serve as the point of reference for the answers to other questions in subsequent chapters. Readers who find themselves particularly struck by a particular answer in later chapters will want to flip back to this one for information about the respondent. Different CASE finalists emphasized different qualities of the teachers who most influenced them. Although no two of us emphasized quite the same qualities, all of us were touched.

Sundays and Sundaes and French

Robert G. Albertson has taught in the religion department and the Asian studies program at the University of Puget Sound in Tacoma, Washington, since 1956. He has participated in the administration of the honors program and the Pacific Rim study and travel program. In this last, he has led study groups to Asia. He was a CASE finalist in 1984:

> Helen McKinney taught more than French. Sunday afternoons were for *causeries* with her students. Her door was open and the tea table was set and the only rule that was enforced was the "French only" language requirement for the afternoon. Helen McKinney taught athletes and fraternity bozos, culture and style, Sundays and sundaes, mores and irregular verbs, and French. And much more.

Unrelenting Gentility

Anthony F. Aveni is professor of astronomy and anthropology at Colgate University in Hamilton, New York. He teaches a variety of courses on solar-system and stellar astronomy, the history of science, astrophysics, and astroarcheology. For more than a decade, he has taken students to Mexico to measure and map the ruins of ancient Mexico in an attempt to discover whether the Mexican pyramids are aligned in ways that give evidence of ancient astronomy. He was named the CASE professor of the year in 1982:

> It has taken me quite some time since I left school to recognize that the teacher I respect most was not my most charismatic or most outgoing professor. Rather, he was a strict disciplinarian, a person who showed me that the problems posed by our attempts to comprehend the natural world are soluble. Ray Weymann was the living example of the instructor who "rides herd" on his students, who does not give up on them, who is not afraid to criticize them—often harshly. He demonstrated for me by his unrelenting gentility that I could solve any problem if I persevered.

Research at an Early Age

William M. Bass III is professor and head of the department of anthropology at the University of Tennessee in Knoxville. As forensic anthropologist for the state of Tennessee, he specializes in the study of human skeletal remains and teaches undergraduate and graduate courses in physical anthropology and forensic anthropology. He was named CASE professor of the year in 1985:

> Clifford C. Evans was a fantastic teacher who gave interesting lectures and required his students to read extensively and to get involved in minor research projects. He would invite students to his home, where he and his wife would show slides and talk about his research in South America. It was exciting, as students, to feel that we were part of the research.

Never Spoke a Word in His Class

Barbara Harrell Carson is an associate professor of English at Rollins College in Winter Park, Florida, where she specializes in American literature. She also teaches composition and introduction to literature. She was a CASE finalist in 1984:

> Robert Lawton taught Shakespeare. I remember his coming into the classroom with meticulously prepared lectures— and then almost never consulting his notes. What he had to say was as focused and as complexly textured as the literature he taught. He seemed to know all the plays, the criticism, the historical background—even the line citations—and it was clear that he loved it all. He was not a demonstrative person. I do not think he ever uttered an "Isn't that terrific!" But his delight in the language and ideas of Shakespeare showed. I never spoke in his class. I hated it when other students did, because it meant less time for him. It surprises me that I think of Robert Lawton as the professor who most influenced me as an undergraduate. My own teaching style is very different from his, because I learned from other good teachers the joys of class discussion, the excitement of ideas bouncing around the classroom from many voices. Maybe his greatest lesson was that there is more than one way to be an effective teacher.

Guided Tours Through a Cell

Mary Eleanor Clark is a professor of biology at San Diego State University, where she teaches physiology, introductory biology, and interdisciplinary course in global issues. She has taught an interdisciplinary course involving ethical dilemmas of modern society, particularly those relating to the use of resources. She was named the first CASE professor of the year in 1981:

> Daniel Mazia's lectures on cell physiology were divine. His word conjured up in my mind the things he was talking about. His lectures were like guided tours through the inside of a cell. Knowledge, enthusiasm, charisma: all were wrapped up together in him. He loved knowing, and he loved anyone who wanted to know.

Do Not Whimper

Kenneth E. Eble is professor of English at the University of Utah in Salt Lake City. He teaches a wide range of courses, from "The Literature of Mountains" to "The Intellectual Tradition of the West." He was a CASE finalist in 1985:

> Gerald Else was a tough teacher but a compassionate one. He was a stimulating teacher but a whole and engaging person. I kept in touch with him. Once I wrote to him seeking sympathy during an arid period of graduate study. He told me not to whimper. It was good advice and helped me become an open and vigorous critic of things I might otherwise have accepted and whimpered about.

The Singing of Caedmon

Sister Maura Eichner, SSND, teaches English at the College of Notre Dame of Maryland in Baltimore. She has been especially interested in the teaching of poetry, short fiction, and Shakespeare. She was a CASE finalist in 1984:

> Frances Smith was one of my great teachers. A member of a teaching congregation of religious, she exemplified a strong Christian tradition of scholarship and contemplation. She taught Anglo-Saxon literature and Chaucer with enthusiasm. "Sing, Caedmon, sing" still speaks to me in her voice. She made me feel as well as think of "The Seafarer," "The Wife's Lament," wisdom in Boethius, language in Bede. With her I tasted irony and laughter in Chaucer. She made me delight in writing papers because she was willing to be excited by the ideas of the young. She believed the best in me and helped me to believe in it and to live by it.

Shaking Hands with Amputated Limbs

Julienne H. Empric is professor of literature at Eckerd College in St. Petersburg, Florida. She teaches Shakespeare, early British literature, history of drama, and women's studies. She chaired the college's interdisciplinary humanities program for freshmen, and she regularly organizes an on-campus forum for monthly discussions of issues and techniques in teaching. She was a CASE finalist in 1983:

> Because the teacher who most influenced me was a combination of good news and bad, he shall here go unnamed. He was brilliant, in an offhand manner. His wit was sharp. His perceptions about literature were incisive. His ability for recall of anecdotal information and humorous asides was unmatched, as was his capacity to appreciate and to stimulate appreciation of the macabre. I recall full class periods on Senecan elements in Renaissance drama—ripped-out hearts, bitten-out tongues, brother-sister incest, handshakes with amputated limbs. He waved his sense of the theatrical like a wand to enthrall the average undergraduate. And his personal magnetism resulted in a cluster of the best students maniacally performing at high levels of achievement in order to gain and retain his approval. This magnetism produced some of the richest interactions I had with fellow majors in literature, for he would regularly cover his lack of preparation by turning class sessions over to students clamoring to perform. Unfortunately, he himself was rarely prepared beyond the general or idiosyncratic material earlier years had provided him. He rarely reread works he assigned, never had written lectures. Despite the good will of avid followers, class "discussion" often dragged interminably and unprofitably. Students began to realize that reading a critical article or seriously considering a play on their own was more profitable than attending class. His influence on me has been formidable. I entered the teaching profession in no small part to make up to another generation for what I had missed in the classes of this teacher. Yet he, more than any other, caused me to confront the potential I have for college teaching, to capitalize on my own sense of seriousness and responsibility, without losing that sense of play that inspires, relieves, enchants.

Baseball and Oyster Stew

Sol Gittleman is the McCollester Professor of Religion at Tufts University in Medford, Massachusetts, where he also serves as provost and senior vice-president. He continues to teach courses on German and Yiddish literature. He was a CASE finalist in 1982:

> John Schabacker was the manager of the baseball team and was also the German department. He saw that I was more than just an infielder, got me to take German, and showed me more kindness than I had ever known. He also showed me how much fun a teacher could have. He was real, he was a friend to his players, a mentor to his students, a genuine companion. He convinced me that I was an intellectual. He took me to the theater, taught me to eat oyster stew, and showed a street kid from Hoboken what life might be like on a college campus for an educator.

Performer and Informer

Robert J. Higgs is professor of English at East Tennessee State University in Johnson City, Tennessee. He teaches courses in American literature, specializing in the literature of Southern Appalachia and the literature of sports. He was a CASE finalist in 1984:

> I can still see and hear R. W. Daly lecturing, especially on the Navy in World War II, showing endless connections between the war and world politics. He always walked when he lectured and had a flair for the dramatic. In addition to describing the Battle of Midway, he would more or less present it by stationing himself at different points in the front of the room and re-creating the aerial combat with his hands in the air before him. He also had a sense of the comic, dropping down before a desk and using his fingers as antiaircraft guns to illustrate some position of defense used by the Japanese. From R. W. Daly, I learned that a teacher is a performer as well as an informer and that we can never have enough knowledge before going into action.

From One to Five-Hundred

Emil T. Hofman is professor of chemistry and dean of the freshman year of studies at the University of Notre Dame in Notre Dame, Indiana. More than 30,000 students have taken his course in general chemistry, and he has helped reduce freshman attrition at Notre Dame to only 1 percent. He was a CASE finalist in 1984:

> In 1946, I returned to college to resume the education I had interrupted for military service in 1942. One of the first

courses I took as a new upperclassman was called "Coordinating Seminar." The teacher was Keith Laidler, one of the foremost physical chemists in the country. I was the only student in the course. I expected to be dazzled by Dr. Laidler's brilliant lectures, but not once during an entire year did he lecture to me. Instead, every Monday, Wednesday, and Friday morning the two of us met in his office, and each meeting concluded with a reading assignment. At the beginning of the next meeting, Dr. Laidler always asked me to discuss what I had read. I would, in effect, deliver the lecture. Periodically he interrupted my presentation to ask a question on material that I apparently did not fully understand. I was disappointed. I had expected to get much more from Dr. Laidler. It was not until I started to teach that I realized how much I really had learned from him. In addition to the chemical knowledge I had derived, I had learned how to learn and how to teach. From my experience in that course, I came to appreciate that the object of education is for the student to learn, and the role of the teacher is somehow to cause that student to learn. For several years I have taught general chemistry to two classes, with five-hundred freshmen in each class. The methods I have used are based on those I experienced with Dr. Laidler in a one-to-one arrangement.

Education in Diversity

Parker G. Marden is the Charles A. Dana Professor of Sociology at St. Lawrence University in Canton, New York. He teaches courses on social issues and policies, on the sociology of health and medicine, on the sociology of the environment, and on equality and inequality in Canada. In recent summers, he has helped to teach a field course on the social, economic, environmental, and cultural problems of the Adirondack and Appalachian regions. He was a CASE finalist in 1984:

> As an undergraduate I was educated and stimulated by a group of teachers who together offered me more than any single professor, however possessed by greatness, could have provided. While I envy those who developed close ties with a mentor or those who were shaped by the example of a strong role model, I think that I am better for my exposure to a collection of men who taught at Bates College in the late 1950s. I feel this way for several reasons. First, there is something powerfully educating in diversity. While my edu-

cation in matters of race and gender was to come later, I had an opportunity to see how men thought and reasoned in different ways. As I look back, Bates College in the 1950s seems provincial, and the curriculum, to quote a present colleague, was dominated by the ideas of dead white men. But to a stripling from a small high school in Massachusetts, it was an exciting bazaar for ideas, and the differences in the vendors offered their own important lessons. Second, most of my teachers set high expectations for me. They provided few places to hide in either the curriculum or the classroom. Third, these men taught me some early lessons about loyalty to a college and to general education. In the 1950s, Bates was a place with a strong core curriculum and various distribution requirements. Good teachers were everywhere and were easily accessible.

Pistol Under His Coat

Kenneth S. Norris is professor of natural history at the University of California, Santa Cruz, where he works both on desert biology and on the study of dolphins and whales. He has directed the center for marine studies and founded the twenty-seven-member natural-area reserve system in California. He teaches courses on the biology of marine mammals, on vertebrate natural history, and on the natural history of California. This last is a field course involving trips to various locations in the state. He was a CASE finalist in 1982:

> Ray Cowles turned my career around just as I was becoming a senior. I went along on one of Cowles's trips to the Mohave Desert. He seemed to know everything, and he carried a romantic explorer's air about him. Born in South Africa of missionary parents, he spoke Zulu, and we got him to speak a few phrases in that curious clacking tongue. He slept with a pistol under his folded coat, a remnant of his days in the Umzumbe Valley of Natal, when such a sidearm would be useful to deal with lions and similar disturbers of the night. But his allure was much more than these momentary revelations. He was obviously buoyed by my questions, and when he answered me he led me down the paths of his own mind. His answers mostly did not come from books. They were instead sharings of his life, his curiosities, his syntheses. And he was amazingly synthetic. He led me down dozens of intellectual trails I had never even thought existed. For him, always, the living thing-in-nature was central.

"The specimen is the authority," he said. If one wanted to learn about nature, one had to block out preconceptions and contrive to look directly at nature's life processes, without injection of any personal bias. That view is utterly central today to all I do. It was he who taught me to see in nature.

He Gave of Himself

Charles E. Ratliff, Jr., is the William R. Kenan, Jr., Professor of Economics at Davidson College in Davidson, North Carolina, where he has taught since 1947. He has also served two short terms with the United Methodist Board of Global Ministries as professor of economics at the Forman Christian College in Pakistan. He was a CASE finalist for 1985:

> As a 16-year-old freshman out of a Southern cotton patch, I was introduced to college mathematics by William G. McGavock with masterful teaching, patience, understanding, and a willingness to give of himself to us students with utmost selflessness. In letters home, I naturally wrote about my courses and professors, and what I said about my math professor is indicated by my mother's comment that she would like to meet "that wonderful Dr. McGavock—he must be the greatest person who ever lived!" This was not a misreading by a freshman. We later served together as faculty colleagues, and his fantastic humaneness and selflessness never dimmed throughout his life.

Stupid Questions Were All Right

Benjamin F. Richason, Jr., is professor of geography at Carroll College in Waukesha, Wisconsin. He teaches courses on physical geography, climatology, cartography, and remote sensing of the environment. He was the first professor in the United States to conduct aerial field trips, and he developed the audiovisual tutorial method in geography. He was a CASE finalist in 1984:

> Thomas F. Barton was a master lecturer. He was entertaining, scholarly, precise, loud, animated, and friendly. I could talk to him in his office, as well as ask stupid questions in the classroom, without fear of being ridiculed or "put down." He was interested in the personal lives of students. He helped me during a difficult time in the birth of our first child. He helped me enter graduate school. He helped me obtain my first college teaching job. He wrote to me fre-

quently when I became a college teacher. Even today, after I have completed what I consider to be a good class session, I think: That is the way Dr. Barton would do it.

Rescued from the Business World

Paul D. Saltman is professor of biology at the University of California at San Diego. His teaching, at both the graduate and undergraduate levels, and his research concern bioinorganic chemistry, cell biology, and the nutrition of trace elements. He served as provost of Revelle College from 1967 to 1972 and as vice-chancellor for academic affairs from 1972 to 1980 at the University of California at San Diego. He was a CASE finalist in 1984:

> James Bonner changed my life. I was intellectually bruised and bloodied by three and a half undergraduate years as a chemistry major. I was turned off to science. I applied to and was accepted by the Harvard School of Business Administration. Science had ceased to be a passion and had become a punishment for me. James Bonner was a professor of biology. I needed an elective and chose his course in plant biochemistry. James bounced into that room on the first day as a model scientist filled with enthusiasm. He was a brilliant scholar, knowledgeable about everything biological and otherwise, and dedicated to communicating his love of science to all who sat before him or worked beside him. In those ten weeks that I was with him in the spring of 1949, he rekindled my excitement in science, challenged me to reach out to my full potential, and gave me literally and figuratively parts of his own self to make part of me. When I decided that I did not want the business school and worldly riches, he welcomed me back and became my mentor. He taught me to suck on a pipette, to ask good questions of nature, to do the quick and dirty experiment, to ski, to fail. But most important, he gave me the unique opportunity to feel fantastic when an experiment works and reveals new insight into the wonder of nature.

Threads of Different Texture

Daniel G. Sisler is professor of agricultural economics at Cornell University in Ithaca, New York. Among the courses he teaches are an introduction to the economics of agricultural geography and graduate seminars in international trade and economic development. His research on the transfer of agricultural technology to low-income countries and on the role of international trade in the process of economic development requires that he make frequent trips to Africa and Asia. He was a case finalist in 1982. Dan Sisler is blind.

> Jay Wiley, a professor of economics at Purdue University, had a tremendous impact on me as an individual and on my decision to become a teacher. I had been blinded in the Air Force and had just returned to Purdue to complete my undergraduate degree. I was confused and uncertain about my future and abilities. Economics in those days was primarily graphics: "If lines don't come tangent or cross, you don't have a solution." Each day, the blackboard was covered with complex graphs, and Professor Wiley had several colors of chalk dust on his coat. He used green for marginal cost, red for marginal revenue, and "the dotted yellow perpendicular to the price axis." I was completely baffled, ready to transfer to a less visual career. Jay Wiley patiently drew the diagrams on my hand and talked me through innumerable graphs. We were getting nowhere. Then he decided to experiment with threads of different texture, yarn, and fish line. We finally settled on the right tactile combinations. Jay Wiley's skill as a teacher, his patience, and his ability to accept the challenge of a different kind of student's needs made the difference. After thirty years, I still have the looseleaf notebook of raised-line diagrams. Jay Wiley sold me on the discipline of economics and provided a tremendous role model as a teacher.

Some of the Most Awful Jokes

Lawrence P. Ulrich is professor of bioethics and chair of the department of philosophy at the University of Dayton, in Dayton, Ohio. His teaching specialties include Marxist philosophy as well as bioethics. He has taught at the University of Dayton since 1964 and currently also holds clinical appointments in the school of medicine and the school of professional psychology at Wright State University. In 1985 he earned his master's degree in counseling and acts as an ethics consultant to three hospitals. He was a CASE finalist in 1984:

> George Berwanger manifested a total dedication to his subject matter and was able to communicate that one indispensable factor for learning—love. His great romance was with Shakespeare, and he communicated that both in and out of

the classroom. He directed a Shakespeare play each year, and it was the high point of the year. He taught so much besides just the literature. He taught us how to communicate, he taught us poise, and most of all he taught us dedication and teamwork. He had a wonderful gift for being able to laugh at himself. He told some of the most awful jokes and created some of the most ludicrous puns, but when he laughed at them he was Jack Benny, Bob Hope, and George Burns all rolled into one. But his laughter did not stop there. He laughed hardest at his own foibles and imperfections. That, of all else, may be the secret of survival as a teacher and as a human being.

The Mathematics of Chemistry

Helen Vendler is professor of English at Harvard University, where she teaches a core course called "Poems, Poets, Poetry," as well as courses in the English and American lyric from the renaissance through the modern period. She is poetry critic for *The New Yorker*. She was a CASE finalist in 1983:

> My freshman year required-science course was taught by a remarkable teacher, Sister Magdalen Julie. She taught chemistry from a mathematical base, with perfect lucidity and with a disarming simplicity. In her hands, analytical problems became the working out of almost self-evident principles. It was my first exposure to being taught mathematical principles by a natively mathematical person. I felt, in that freshman chemistry class, not that I was learning chemistry (although I was) but that I was being taught to think (and I was). In the course in organic chemistry, also taught by Sister Magdalen Julie, she reduced the wilderness of organic chemistry to visible principles and conveyed her own deep interest in the enormously complex interactions possible in organic equations.

In a sense, of course, all good teachers teach organic chemistry, that special bonding of one living organism to another. No two of these teachers sound quite alike, but they all discovered the power to touch that all good teachers know, and they all showed by their examples how others might also touch.

College teaching takes place in an ivory tower, yet the best professors agree with remarkable unanimity that their jobs are intimately and directly connected with the real world outside the walls of the tower.

"Our Best Classes Are Life Classes": The Real World and the College Classroom

Teaching is a real-world activity. Although we professors are in some ways isolated and insulated by our office walls and laboratory walls and classroom walls from the world of cash and cutthroats and cosmopolites, we are very much involved, through our research and our teaching, in the realities and needs of that wider world.

Self-Reliance and Rejection Slips

I have always been uncomfortable with certain features of the ivory tower. Part of my discomfort with the ivory tower has to do with my responsibility to my students and to society. Teaching a subject like English has sometimes made me feel irresponsible. I have all these fresh young people in my classes. I know that virtually all of them will one day be out in some real-world situation where they have to provide some service or produce some commodity to earn a living, yet I spend my time with them introducing Chaucer's Wife of Bath or inviting them to try their hands at writing poems or encouraging them to notice that most effective expository paragraphs do have topic sentences.

P. G. Beidler (ed.). *Distinguished Teachers on Effective Teaching.*
New Directions for Teaching and Learning, no. 28. San Francisco: Jossey-Bass, Winter 1986.

Occasionally I feel the need to justify myself to my students in real-world terms. I tell them that the skills they develop in analyzing the Wife of Bath will be of use to them in the corporate setting, where they will have to know how to understand, from a few apparently disconnected hints of behavior, what makes people run. I tell them that the creativity they draw on, and learn to trust in when they write poetry, will be of use to them when they raise children who refuse to follow any rules of human nature except their own. I tell them that by learning to focus their paragraphs, they will be better prepared to use effectively the 30 percent of their time that, as typical college-educated professionals, they will spend on the job doing writing-related tasks.

Occasionally I pay more direct homage to the real world by teaching experimental courses, in which I take my students right out into it. One semester, for example, I taught a course called "Self-Reliance in a Technological Society." In that course, fifteen undergraduates and I formed a corporation—a real one, registered in Harrisburg—with me as president and them as members of the board of directors. We got a bank loan, purchased a run-down house near the university, and spent the semester renovating it. This was all part of an upper-level English course in which we read Thoreau's *Walden* and a half-dozen other books, kept journals, and wrote term papers. At the end of the course, we sold the house at a $3000 profit, paid half of that to the government as corporate income taxes, distributed the rest among the students, and dissolved the corporation.

Later—to give one more example—I taught another course oriented to the real world. The name of the course was "Writing Fiction for *Redbook*." I selected *Redbook* because it was the best fiction market for young writers in America. The only texts for the course were recent issues of *Redbook* magazine. We spent class time talking about what *Redbook* stories had in common: Was there always a love interest? How were women portrayed? Was there an attempt at humor? Did the stories end happily? (We found, incidentally, that there was such richness in the stories that we could make almost no universal generalizations about them.) We then set about trying to write stories good enough to be accepted for publication in *Redbook*. In doing so, we were motivated not by the grades that are the only pay for stories in traditional creative writing courses, but by the $850 that *Redbook* paid for the first stories by new authors. In the end, we all sent our best efforts to New York for editorial review. And in the end, we all received rejection slips because none of us was able to write well enough to be published. We were all disappointed, of course, but we had all learned one of the important lessons that the real world has to offer to serious would-be fiction writers: It is easier to get an A in a college course than to write well enough to get a story accepted by a national magazine.

I could give more examples. I could tell about the time I took my freshman English students on a wilderness trip for two days in an effort to give them something interesting to write about. I could tell about the time I took some students in a course about the Hopi Indians to Arizona for a week to live and work on the Hopi reservation. I have said enough, however, to show how hard I have tried to connect my courses and my students with the real world. It was natural enough, then, that when I wrote the questions for this book I would ask the CASE finalists this question:

> **To what extent do you try to focus your teaching and the attention of your students on the "real world" beyond the ivory tower? How, as a college teacher, do you view your responsibility to society?**

The responses to this question were more nearly unanimous, more nearly harmonious, than for any other question. The consensus was clear: College teachers have a definite responsibility to put their students in contact with the world outside the academy.

What a Dreadful Question

For some of the CASE finalists, the answer was so obvious that it was almost an annoyance that I asked the question:

> What a dreadful question to ask a sociologist. It is clearly my task to bring my attention, and that of my students, fully to bear on the world that surrounds the college or university. For my part, I take my specific charge from a dictum offered by C. Wright Mills (*The Sociological Imagination*, 1959): "It is the political task of the social scientist—as a liberal educator—continually to translate personal troubles into public issues, and public issues into the terms of their human meaning for a variety of indiviuals." I have to acquaint students with the forces that shape their lives and those of others, especially those of social classes, races, and ethnic backgrounds whom they might never meet, without losing sight of the fact that the consequences of those forces are very real and personal. Fortunately, I get to search for answers in the company of colleagues who ask less worldly questions or help students to understand the issues of the present with the perspectives of the past. I can think of no one so ill prepared as a student in sociology trained only by sociologists. Here is the justification for holding classes in the ivory tower [Marden].

The question by its very nature arouses enormous resentment and nausea in me. The university is the real world. I am an integral part of the real world. I make no attempt toward detachment. To do so would be suicidal and obscene, both for me and for the institution. I cannot read our catalogue, either in the undergraduate or graduate programs, and find a single course that I cannot relate directly or indirectly to the physical and metaphysical phenomena of this planet upon which we so precariously live. I teach every course with reality in mind. My examinations, be they in introductory biology or advanced biochemistry, always include articles from the popular press concerning "real problems" to which a student must apply both knowledge and critical thought to answer effectively. I have an enormous personal responsibility to society. I am an integral part of that society. Were it not for that society, I would not be indulged and supported in this university. I have a great debt to repay [Saltman].

There is no reason an ivory tower should separate students and faculty from the real world. Athens and Sparta and the war that destroyed them are the real world, albeit some centuries in the past. The more I teach, the more I am convinced of the essential relatedness of everything. My responsibility more and more becomes opposing separateness, showing relationships. Having such a view, it seems absurd for me to pursue or pass on compartmentalized knowledge. Teachers are in service to the society that supports them, and I see no great conflict with a sense of service to mankind [Eble].

I do not believe that AT&T's closing average is more real than Plato's *Republic* or more significant than the analysis of antiforeign sentiment in America in the 1920s or the study of the role of the mitochondria in the human cell. The liberal arts liberate us by freeing us from too narrow a definition of reality. In her *One Writer's Beginnings*, Eudora Welty describes her shock when she walked into an art class her first year at college and discovered not a bowl of fruit but "a live human being" who dropped her robe and stood naked before the class. The same year, Welty took a literature course. It, too, she said, was "a life class." If we are especially favored by the gods, our best classes will also be life classes. We will be able to bring Keats or Nietzsche or the family patterns of the !Kung into our classrooms live, and our students will be able to walk all around them and see them breathe. If we can occasionally pull this off, our students (the ones, at any rate, who are themselves alive) will not ask questions about how our subjects relate to the real world or about our responsibility to society [Carson].

Something to Eat Comparatively Recently

For some of the CASE finalists, preparing students for life in the real world is built right into the subject matter or into their own natural approaches to their subjects:

I can hardly avoid focusing on the "real world" in teaching economics, for economics is about bread in the broadest sense. Man does not live by bread alone, but, in the words of the British economist Philip Wicksteed, "A man can be neither a saint, nor a lover, nor a poet, unless he has comparatively recently had something to eat." The study of how society determines what is produced, the way it is produced, and who gets it is pretty "real." Furthermore, since I agree with the neoclassical economist Alfred Marshall that the "chief and . . . highest interest" of economics is to address the problem of poverty, which causes "the degradation of a large part of mankind," the students' attention is inevitably directed through the ivory tower windows to the world outside [Ratliff].

I take seriously Plato's belief that the teacher has a social obligation to communicate knowledge to others so that they will be improved as human beings. To detach oneself from the world is to one-dimensionalize the self. My specialty is bioethics, and it would be easy to talk only about the issues raised in that area, without involvement in the clinical situation. But I see my knowledge and my ability to communicate and relate to others as a gift that I must nurture, and so I have become involved in the arena of medical practice. I am an ethics consultant in several hospitals, and I counsel both patients who suffer from terminal cancer and families who have difficulty coping with the disease. I have just received a degree in counseling to further enhance my clinical work. This activity breathes life into my area of specialization and into my classes. My students benefit much more because of my experience than they ever did before. How can they be expected to take responsible roles in society if I, who encourage them, do not give adequate example [Ulrich]?

I have difficulty separating teaching from public service. Because I am a forensic anthropologist who identifies decayed bodies or skeletons for law enforcement agencies, I make public service a part of my work. I have always believed that the students in my classes, including my large introductory human-origins class, should be kept abreast of the research and applications I am involved in at the moment. Sometimes students think that anthropology deals only with the past. I show them that many anthropological techniques are used to solve modern-day problems [Bass].

In my beginning course, I attempt to paint the nebulous discipline of economics with a broad brush. A part of the class is theory, but to make the theory stick, I tie it to real-world problems. I develop these problems early in the course and add to them throughout the semester, building an increasingly complex framework for understanding various dimensions of economics. My examples, reading, and home-work assignments do not have any obvious tie to a career, but they get students started in their thinking that the acquisition of knowledge is important in that it helps us to formulate problems and seek solutions to them [Sisler].

Part of my responsibility to society consists in helping my students to reveal their own biases. I try to do this in my astronomy course, for example, by exploring the degree to which we can look objectively at Stonehenge, that great monument constructed 5,000 years ago, and try to understand it in terms of our knowledge of the culture that built it. We talk about why they built it and for what purpose they used it. We try hard to avoid assuming that our own cultural traits were also those of these ancient people. I try to raise the question "Are modern astronomers really erecting card-board ancestors of themselves when they see in Stonehenge alignments and calculations relating to the heavens?" Our study becomes a lesson in the limits of our own ethnocentrism [Aveni].

Everything that I teach is intended to connect to the lives of my students. I try to make them find their location somewhere on the spectrum I create in class. I concentrate on two subject areas, and both come out of my personal background, my own life. I teach a course called "From Shtetl to Suburbia: An Introduction to Yiddish Culture." This course is an intellectual expression of my own life as a child of European Jewish immigrants. Together, my students and I look back and try to give our lives a historical context. I do the same thing in my other courses, which deal with the rise of Hitler in Nazi Germany. My context: a century of total war. We read the literature associated with German culture from the time of Nietzsche and Wagner right up to the World War II era and beyond, in order to explain the causes of two wars and the need to avoid a third. I feel the responsibility to make my courses important in the lives of my students. I want to make a difference. I want my students to feel changed after fourteen weeks [Gittleman].

Out There in Some Wash

Several of the CASE finalists reported that they did their best teaching when they took their students away from the traditional classroom:

Although I am able when lecturing to excite students with my personal enthusiasm and knowledge, my best teaching by far is in nature, where I become an orchestrator of events for students. Out there in some wash, or on a flower-covered hillside, I contrive the circumstances that confront the student directly with some process or event in nature. By thus standing aside, I can cause students to discover for themselves. And then the most banal fact comes alive with the force of personal discovery. For instance, when I ask my students to spend an entire day with a single organism, each student trying to psych out its conditions for life by hunkering down with a lily or a spider, the most amazing skeins of discovery unfold. Then, when the day is over, we share our minirevelations. Almost always there is a chatter of sharing and excitement, as the students wander toward each other with such words as "I noticed that wild cucumber business, how they hold on to other plants with those little springs, those coiled tendrils, so no wind can blow them away" or "Did the ravens really turn over boards to find insects? Can you show me?" Out in the field, also, my students can see me in unrehearsed action, learning and doing and failing. Out there, they have the chance to say, "If that old white-haired gink can try, and then laugh when things get tough, and then try again, why can't I?" [Norris].

As a geographer, I attempt on a daily basis to bring the real world into the classroom. What students learn in geography occurs in real places—places where people have different social values, different religions, different mores, different languages, different economic conditions, and different ways of making a living. Facts, concepts, and relationships are meaningless unless students know the places in which these elements of the natural and cultural environments are located. I have tried to facilitate their knowing about such places by developing what I call the audiovisual-tutorial independent method of learning. Each of my taped discussions is accompanied by slides I have taken of places, landforms, atmospheres, people, workplaces, villages, cities, maps, and diagrams. Through these, my geography students are constantly exposed to the referent world. As one student put it,"I feel that I have been there." But that is not the same as really being there, and I have also taken my students on field trips—to the Rockies, to the desert Southwest, to Europe, and to the West Indies—to provide them with real-life experiences in a totally different physical environment. I have also conducted field trips by air, so that my students can see for themselves the total mosaic of the land, with the woof of the landforms interwoven with the warp of the cultural patterns. There is life beyond the classroom, and my students learn that both from the air and on the ground [Richason].

I have tried to make "openness" a contagious disease by exposing students, colleagues, and family to new places, ideas, and persons. With Aileen and our children, I have taken Easter recesses in San Francisco, thus exposing a community of learners to the urbane, strange, exciting city on the bay, to some of its social problems, and to some of the people working with those problems in ghettoes, Chinatown, the Tenderloin, suburbs, courthouses. I also helped initiate an Asian studies program to transform the Pacific Ocean from a barrier to a bridge. Aileen and I dramatized the new curriculum with a series of nine-month study-travel programs to nine Asian countries. To be "responsible" to society seems to require some "irresponsible" behavior: Neglecting committee assignments, common-sense security, dependable colleagues, and the fruits of predictability. It is to be gone as much as to be around [Albertson].

The Liberal Arts Seem Meaningless

A number of CASE finalists answered the question from the broader perspective of what a liberal education is all about:

> My responsibility to society is to assist young people to become competent in their chosen fields and to become liberally educated, so that they themselves can construct on an intellectual basis the values that will guide them throughout life [Hofman].

> Converging economic, political, and environmental events—not to mention the arms race—are creating incredible global pressures that our students will have to deal with in their lifetimes. Most of them are vaguely aware of this but prefer not to think about it. They would rather see themselves as clients coming to college to be molded for a secure niche in the megamachine of our economy. As such, a majority of my students are impatient with learning "unnecessary" basic skills and are often bored with science, philosophy, or literature because these subjects do not clearly speak to their immediate goals. The liberal arts seem meaningless in our pragmatic, self-centered society. Yet it is precisely in these disciplines, if properly approached, that the questions and problems that exist in today's world can best be addressed. In my experience in biology, at least, when survey subjects are taught so that they throw light on contemporary questions and issues, students are immediately interested. Nor does such teaching trivialize the subject; on the contrary, it stimulates a deeper interest to learn more. Finally, it creates a bond between student and teacher, since the teacher is clearly concerned about the world that her or his students will live in [Clark].

> I teach in a liberal arts college where one discipline touches another, meshes with it, and becomes, paradoxically, a great net to hold an infinite number of questions, and at the same time to release possibilities, intuitions, sometimes even answers to the problems of the "real world." Do Dante and Shakespeare really lead us from the "real world" [Eichner]?

There Must Be Great Audiences, Too

Dante and Shakespeare, indeed. Questions about the connections between the college classroom and the real world, of course, have special meaning for those of us who teach literature. These days, we are often put on the defensive by our students and by our colleagues in more "practical" fields. Just why should we ask that students study literature, when there are more immediately relevant subjects to study—accounting, computers, engineering, marketing? Here are some answers from literature professors:

> My responsibility to society is to teach students to develop and refine their abilities to think, feel, read, write, and speak. The last three skills should be adequate to express the increasing dimensions of the first two capacities, thinking and feeling. I am committed to the value of liberal arts education, and so the "material" through which these abilities are learned and practiced should most often be primary texts of proven and perennial worth—the classics of literature, philosophy, and history. I do, however, believe strongly in the value of analogy as a teaching tool and so I enlist regular and multiple references to relevant current situations and contemporary problems. In my course "Woman as Metaphor," readings include passages from the Bible, but we also read and discuss selections of modern poetry offering Biblical women as contemporary metaphors. And we read newspaper and journal articles on sexism in Biblical language, or in favor of equal status for Eve, or debating the admission of women into ministries and priesthoods. In several courses, I require real-world projects ("What classic comic situations can you observe in one hour's time in a shopping mall?"). Or we work together to "people" great literature with figures from current soap opera or film or political science ("Who would best depict the Wife of Bath, as you understand Chaucer's characterization of her: Joan Collins? Meryl Streep? the registrar? Margaret Thatcher?") [Empric].

I do not look upon the classroom as an ivory tower or an "unreal" place, any more than I look upon ball games as "make believe." I do not emphasize the difference between the reality outside the classroom and that inside. Instead, I concentrate on similarities. I tell my freshmen and sophomores that explicating a poem is much like looking at a car that one is thinking of buying. Although a poem and a car are very different, some crucial questions are the same in evaluating them. Does the poem or car work as advertised? How does it work? What are the important features of the poem or in the decision to purchase the car? How does the poem or car reflect my relationship with nature and society?

Instead of distinguishing between the "real world" and the "ivory tower," I use the terms "useful" and "useless." A car for example, is "useful" and a poem is "useless." Poetry, remember, "makes nothing happen." "Useless," though, also means "priceless," and for that reason, the values they reflect should have a bearing on future decisions our graduates make [Higgs].

Since I teach poetry, I encounter more often the problem of teaching my students to focus on the art of the poem as well as on its subject. They see quite readily that Keats is upset by the ills of existence. They see less readily that an ode has a contour by which they can trace Keat's experience of such ills, a set of images by which he exemplifies his reactions, a stanza calling certain genres to mind, a form borrowed from the tradition of prayer and invocation, and so on. The constant back-and-forth—between the aspect of life and its treatment by art—that the teacher of poetry must undertake ensures that many aspects of "life" are brought up for discussion. I also discuss the social uses of art, its use as a vehicle of nationalist expression, and its use as a vehicle of ethnicity. I point out the absence of certain voices (female, black) before such groups were given the education needed for the writing of poetry, and the absence of certain subjects (childbirth, daughterhood) in the presence of other subjects (war, sonship). How do I, as a college teacher, view my responsibility to society? I would like to help provide an audience at home with poetry, so that our poets will have someone to write for (Whitman: "To have great poetry, there must be great audiences, too"). Poetry used to be taught in the schools, but less and less does that seem to be so. It would be better if students encountered poetry from their earliest days, but if that is not to be, at least they should encounter it before they leave college. I especially want them to know that their society contains living poets addressing issues that are important to them, and that there exists a form of beauty that satisfies, very deeply, readers to whom the play of language is a form of joy [Vendler].

Those who can, do; those who do, teach. Through field trips to the Rockies, through police reports about the clues hidden in the decayed body of a murder victim, through discussions about the original uses of Stonehenge, through personal anecdotes about a teacher's childhood, through proofs that the play of language is a form of joy, good teachers demonstrate their conviction that they perform a real and useful function for society. Most of us, it seems, have never wasted much time wondering whether what we do in the college classroom is important in the so-called real world beyond it. If that were not a given of our vocation as college teachers, we would perhaps be doing something different with our lives.

Research, scholarship, and writing are important to the profession, but only if they are kept in proper proportion, if they ultimately serve the needs of the students, and if the university provides adequate time for them.

"A Privilege, Not an Obligation": Research, Scholarship, and the Needs of Students

Teaching, at least at the college level, is a multiservice profession. It involves serving the educational needs of classrooms full of students, to be sure, but it also involves service to the university and service to the wider professional community. This third kind of service, usually known as research or scholarship, is both the enduring joy and the enduring frustration of professors interested in the welfare of students.

Reading, Talking, and Writing

Back in the mid-sixties, when I was still a graduate student, I decided that it was silly to write all those course papers, get them back with grades and slender comments, and then file them uselessly away. I decided to take some of the comments seriously and revise one of the course papers I most enjoyed working on. Revision meant recasting my argument so that it sounded more like those in the articles I had been forced to read as preparation for writing the paper. It meant sounding more self-assured than I felt, removing expressions like "I think" and "or

P. G. Beidler (ed.). *Distinguished Teachers on Effective Teaching.*
New Directions for Teaching and Learning, no. 28. San Francisco: Jossey-Bass, Winter 1986.

so it seems to me." It meant referring to other scholars, not when they were right but when they were sufficiently wrong to convince a journal editor that the world needed to hear my more correct view. I retyped the article on my old Olympia manual typewriter and sent it out. Six months later, I got a letter of rejection. I reread my paper, gave it a better title, made a few small revisions, and sent it to another journal. I still remember the thrill I felt when the letter came—another six months later—saying that the article had been accepted for publication. And I still remember the thrill I felt—a lesser thrill, but a thrill nevertheless—when much later I got my first offprints. I was not inclined to reread the article when the offprints came out, and I was not sure what I was going to do with twenty-five of them, but holding them in my hand and seeing my name on them was glorious fun. I was glad that by then I had sent out a few more of my seminar papers, properly revised to make them look like the work of a competent scholar.

After I finished my dissertation on Chaucer, collected my degree, and taught full-time for a year, I was so tired of words and ideas that I asked for and received a year's leave of absence, without pay, from my teaching job. That year, I supported my wife and two small children as a carpenter. It was a good year, an exhilarating year, but I found myself after a while spending my evenings rereading my dissertation. That was a dreary experience, but I discovered in doing so that in there among all the degree-getting words there were some original and right ideas that other scholars really ought to know about. It was satisfying to make that discovery.

I rewrote those ideas as four articles. One by one, they were accepted. Returning to my teaching job, I realized all of a sudden that I really was a scholar. As those articles came out, one by one, I saw that I was taking part in a scholarly conversation with other scholars, men and women I had never met but with whom I shared a common reading list and a common interest. Then one day I read my name in a footnote in someone else's article. I smiled. It was as if I were taking part—in slow motion, of course—in a discussion class, a seminar. It was fun.

I started keeping an "article possibilities" file. Whenever I taught a work of literature, I developed ideas about how to interpret it. Some of these ideas sounded pretty good as I discussed them with my students. When I felt that I might have kicked loose from the sand a little gem of what might be a publishable idea or interpretation, I jotted it down and put it into my file. Then, when summer came, I got out my "article possibilities" file and sorted through it. Most of the gems looked pretty ordinary or dull by then, but a few of them still sparkled. I went to the library and poked around in bibliographies to see if any of the titles indicated that someone else might have found my little gem. I remember how surprised I was to discover how quickly I could skim a book if I knew what I was hoping to find—or, more usually, hoping not to find. Some of my gems panned out, and I wrote them up and sent them out. It was fun.

One day, just before Christmas, my department chairperson invited me to come into his office. He closed the door. He just wanted me to know, he said, that although I was only in my fourth year at Lehigh, the department was recommending me for promotion and tenure. He explained that they did not usually put people up early, but he had heard good things about my teaching, and the department was impressed with my publications activity. I was pleased, of course, but I remember being surprised that he referred to my sending out those articles as "publications activity" to be rewarded with a promotion. I had done that writing for fun, for the thrill of discovering that others in my field might actually want to read some of my ideas about literature.

I realize now that I was incredibly naive in those days, and that probably everyone in the department assumed that I had been working so hard at writing because I wanted to publish my way into an early promotion. I am less naive now, but I still write and publish mostly for the fun of it, and I am delighted to be in a profession that pays me to do things that are so satisfying—reading literature, talking with students, and publishing. Reading, talking, and publishing are closely interrelated. Reading literature is preparation for talking with students who have read the same literature. Knowing I will be talking with students forces me to prepare, to work out questions and ideas about literature. Talking about those questions and ideas with students helps me to see relationships more clearly, and that sometimes makes me want to write about them so that I can share them in a more permanent medium with a wider audience. Reading, talking, and publishing are all different, all worth doing in themselves, but this profession of mine pays me to do what comes naturally: having fun making the three work together to enrich each other.

Did others professors, I wondered, see a symbiotic relationship between teaching and publishing? Here is how I put the question to the other CASE finalists:

> **How do you personally view the obligation most professors have to do scholarship and research, get grants, and publish, in addition to teaching students?**

The answers to this questions ranged broadly, but most of the CASE finalists felt strongly that scholarship and research, at least if interpreted broadly to mean "keeping up with developments in one's field," were necessary parts of the professors's professional life.

The Yin and Yang of My Life

For a few—but only a few—of the CASE finalists, research and scholarship were unquestionably an integral feature of the life of a college professor:

How can I teach if I do not learn? How can I learn if I do not teach? Scholarship and pedagogy are the yin and yang of my life. I try to bring as much creativity to my teaching as I do to my research. These two functions are not polarized and incompatible endeavors. For me, they are one and the same. They are integrated and united. My scholarship gives me a "union card" that admits me to the highest international circles of research scholarship in biology, chemistry, and medicine. It makes me a "desirable character" as a consultant to industry. It allows me to share and understand the frontiers of basic research, their applicaton in medicine, and their technological exploitation. I bring that frontier into my daily classroom existence. Were I not part of that scholarly community, I would be teaching second- and third-derivative science. This way, I not only get students out on the frontier through a theoretical perspective, but I also actually invite them into my laboratory to be part of our research endeavor. Nothing is more wonderful than to let students see their names in print as part of a published article in which they have played a crucial role. How can I be a good human model of a scientist if I am not truly a member of the scientific community of scholars [Saltman]?

I have always had difficulty separating teaching from research and from public service. Good teachers need to do research. If they do research, they should share it, not only with their students but also with the public. All people who enter academic life should have some interest in doing research in their fields. They do not need large grants to do research, but a professor who does not do research cannot be so enthusiastic about his field. Professors should do more than read and interpret the textbook to the student [Bass].

In twenty-six years of teaching, I have never known an exceptional teacher who was a sloppy researcher or writer. Great teachers need to make teaching the centerpiece of their academic careers. They must dedicate at least half their time to excellence in teaching and be confident that this excellence will be observed and rewarded. The balance of their professional time can be extremely productive in research. It is possible to be an exceptional teacher and still conduct solid research. I never work on lecture material for more than three days a week. Three days a week I write, do research, and work with my graduate students. One day a week I have a ball [Sisler].

Research and the Consuming Scholar

Most of the respondents were more temperate, insisting that research and scholarship are important for our profession but not everyone needs actively to do them. For some, it may be enough to keep up with what is done by others:

> The connection between teaching and research is strong, because there is a dynamic between the ever-changing discipline and the individual. Professors who are not involved in some way with the vanguard of their disciplines will produce only sets of yellowed notes they will consult and teach from, year after year. It is too easy for such professors to become stale. But research ought not to be equated with one's ability to generate the printed page. I know a number of "consuming scholars," who do not publish much yet who do keep up very well with their disciplines. These people, although not involved directly in research, understand what is going on because they confer with the people doing the research. I would not want to discredit my colleagues who, although they may not be getting the biggest grants and going to the biggest research universities during the summer, nevertheless are of great value to my university [Aveni].

> Ideally, a college professor should be both a productive researcher and an effective teacher. Research and teaching, however, require very different skills. A brilliant researcher can be a poor teacher, and a highly regarded teacher may do only pedestrian research. A good college or university should welcome to its faculty a person who excels in teaching but is not a productive researcher. But it should also welcome a person who excels in research but is not an effective teacher. It is important, however, that professors do participate in research, if for no other reason than to stay alive in their fields [Hofman].

> It is impossible to remain an effective teacher without good scholarship. At the beginning of their careers, young professors are working with borrowed capital—the knowledge acquired in graduate education. This material must be continually renewed if teaching, packaged as it is into individual courses, is to remain fresh and effective. In this sense, scholarship and publication are not necessarily synonymous.

Not all good teachers need to contribute new insights into the knowledge bases of their disciplines, but they do need to remain fully acquainted with them. One of the major problems in assessing promise and continued growth in academic careers is our inability to assess scholarly potential in support of good teaching apart from the number and heft of publications. The use of "success in publishing" in decisions on tenure and promotion penalizes the truly effective teacher whose scholarly learning directly supports a set of wide teaching interests. Research for publication narrows. Scholarship for teaching expands [Marden].

There are many roads to successful teaching. Getting grants and publishing are certainly effective ways of achieving the goal. There are many other ways that are not so spectacular. It is important that the professor remain current. But professors can do that in ways that are not so spectacular or dramatic. There is no one mold for being a success in the academic community. I suppose that the best one can do is find one's strengths and nurture them [Ulrich].

Had We but World Enough and Time

Some professors consider research and publication to be just fine in an ideal world, but the real world of the academy has students in it, students who need attention. These professors feel so caught up in their teaching and advising duties that they can do research and writing only in blocks of time set off from preparing courses and teaching:

So long as the research and writing activities can be relegated to time that does not belong to a teacher's students, those scholarly pursuits are quite beneficial to teacher and students. In fact, some scholarly research and writing are absolutely necessary to keep a teacher "alive." Since in my institution we teach a full load, regardless of the paper-pushing administrative and committee chores placed upon us, and since we have an open-door policy regarding working with students on an individual basis, I have been able to publish a modest list of items only by using summers, holiday periods, and sabbaticals [Ratliff].

On professional productivity, I have this to say, with apologies to Andrew Marvell:

Had we but world enough, and time,
These expectations were no crime.
My grants and books and texts would grow
Vaster than empires (if more slow).
For scholarship deserves this state,
Nor would I write as lower rate.
But at my back I always hear
A desp'rate student hovering near.

For the teacher who cares about student learning, the seduction of the here-and-now must necessarily be strong. If I could fantasize a semester in which none of my students was ready to learn except in the very ways my courses were prepared to teach them, I might claim half my time for research. There are never such semesters, however, and teaching at a small college adds more complications. I am responsible for a wide range of courses and many committee and curricular assignments. And while fewer students might seem to represent less work, quite the opposite is true: Academic advising becomes "mentoring," with all the benefits of the fuller student-teacher relationship, and all the extra investment of time. And so, the shorter the publications list, the slimmer the chance of gaining funding for released time to conduct research for publication. Keeping abreast of the reading in some of the areas for which I am responsible is one of my chief joys. Writing about some of my ideas must be relegated to summers, holidays, and leaves [Empric].

The administrations in many universities have unrealistic expectations of faculty, who are obligated to teach, do research, and perform service. These expectations are especially unrealistic in state regional universities and especially in the humanities. We all know that students are the victims of the process, since teaching is the easiest of the three activities to abuse, research and service being relatively easy to document. I believe that research and service are important, but released time should be provided for them [Higgs].

I have had a limited number of grants to teach special workshops and to give myself time for writing. Applying for grants takes time that I sometimes begrudge, but I have published consistently, a small but steady output. The time I have spent on this kind of writing has helped me to be a better teacher [Eichner].

36

Writing as Natural as Breathing

One ugly way to answer the question of how much research or scholarship we professors do is through dollars: "She brought in nearly $90,000 last year." Another is pages: "He has averaged forty-five pages a year since 1980." Many serious professors question the appropriateness of either measure. Even many of those who write easily and voluminously question the appropriateness of using writing as a measure of professorial performance. To do so can transform a natural and loving act into a slavish and meaningless one:

> There are three sorts of college teachers: the ones who are natural writers, to whom writing is as natural as breathing, and who also teach; the ones who are natural teachers and to whom writing is foreign and difficult; and the ones who are teachers and who can write on demand. Only the first type should be writing. It is enough if the other two sorts only teach. I do not believe writing should be forced out of people. That only makes for bad writing. Many excellent teachers "do scholarship and research." They read books, read journals, read ancillary works of criticism, read widely in fields outside their own; but they are not prompted by that reading to write things for other people to read. Their classes benefit from their reading, of course, but they do not have the polemic or expressive instincts to publish what they learn from their reading. Often, writing is laborious or unnatural to them. I do not know the solution to this problem. In the past, the solution was more or less that the people who wanted to be chiefly teachers taught in colleges, while the people who wanted to publish taught in universities. This is still partially the case, but publishing requirements have been inflated in both places [Vendler].

Publishing is one of several requirements of promotion, tenure, and satisfactory three-year evaluations. Teaching and advising students are first and second. Research and writing come next. I feel obliged to keep abreast of current scholarship in my field and would feel better about myself if I wrote and published more. But that obligation is not my first priority. Then, too, what is "writing?" I write scores of letters of recommendation for students and colleagues, lectures and talks for the campus and wider community, book reviews for study clubs, and no books [Albertson].

The Grip of the Grant Gods

Some professors feel strongly that this profession of ours has turned a good thing into a potentially destructive thing, particularly when money is involved or when it appears that we are so caught up in the minutiae of scholarship and research that we lose sight of our larger obligations:

> Because I share the process of discovery with my students, rather than merely reciting facts from somebody else's trove, there is no question that in the normal course of events I should discover things. Nor is there any question that I should go about my process of discovery in a professional way. I must know the nature of proof, or else I cannot tell anyone else how it works. But this is not to say that my scholarship must be built according to some stereotyped model. My science seems very human to me, full of everything people are made of. I eschew nothing that lets me see. But the larger universities are clearly in the grip of the grant gods. I once tried to go a couple of years without a grant of any kind, so that I could think and write. It all seemed very logical and scholarly to me, but from my administrators I began to hear hushed voices: "He's kind of old. Do you think he can get a grant any more?" There needs to be a balance struck that will allow our educational institutions to keep their hired intellectuals alive and ticking while the slavish pursuit of research dollars keeps the regents' opportunity coffers filled [Norris].

For scientists, scholarship is almost always taken to mean experimental research, in field or laboratory, and prolific publication of the results of that research. Promotion and tenure are tied to the quality of one's teaching. While I think it is extremely important that every university science teacher have first-hand experience doing original research, it seems to me that the emphasis in this direction has gone overboard in recent years. Two things have happened as a result. Science teaching has been given shorter and shorter shrift. Only upper-division and graduate courses "count," and the fewer even of those one teaches, the better. And today, when more than ever someone should be thinking about and then teaching about the moral issues raised by our ever more powerful science and technology, most scientists at colleges and universities are far too busy "at the cutting edge," churning out data, to bother reflecting on where our discipline is headed [Clark].

As an academic obligation, scholarship is depressing. The forces that drive it, its relationship to academic careers, the lack of critical judgments of its worth, and the deceptions and hypocrisies through which it flourishes make the specific manifestations of scholarship even more depressing. An eminent and much-published scholar, who was a teacher I looked up to because he *was* a scholar, now calls it "scholarship." Yet there is something praiseworthy in it, maybe lodged more in the way it manifests the questioning human mind than what it produces. I speak from the viewpoint of the humanities, which have become inhumane from an excess of scholarship. The sciences, which can show so much material achievement from scholarship, also must accept the stunning achievement of mankind's bringing into the world the power to destroy itself. As to the particulars of the questions of research and teaching, academics should make some simple distinctions. First, scholarship and published research are not the same thing. The former might be an expectation of all teachers and the latter a specialized and idiosyncratic occupation of some. Second, there is no clear relationship between excellent teaching and excellent scholarship, and an even less clear one between excellent teaching and published scholarship. The studies that have been done indicate that excellent scholars can be poor teachers as well as excellent ones and that poor scholars (as determined by conventional academic measures) can be excellent teachers as well as poor ones. Third, the measures used to reward and shape academic careers strongly favor published research, without any careful attention either to the overall aims of education or to the specific needs of students. I think I can fairly and objectively say that I am an academic freak. I am compulsive about writing, but I do not fool myself by claiming that this activity fits hand-in-glove with my teaching. In short, what I am saying is that published research is a monkey on the back that could well be removed without destroying that more important need scholars feel to expand their own and their students' learning. Published scholarship in the humanities has clearly led to a perception on the part of many faculty members that communicating in print with other scholars in a narrow specialty is the purpose of the university and of far greater importance than teaching classes. It is that perversion of values that bothers me most [Eble].

And Not a Little Guilt

The need for scholarship, research, and publication is felt both by professors who engage in them and those who do not. For many, the need is a positive one, encouraging them to do what they enjoy doing and what they entered this profession in part to do:

> There is painful conflict here for me, because I enjoy teaching more than research and writing. I am better at it, and I get more praise for what I do in the classroom than for what I do in print. It strikes me as nearly impossible to be the kind of teacher I want to be, have the family life I value, *and* be the kind of published scholar at the frontiers of the profession that my professors at Johns Hopkins had in mind when they trained me. So the tension is always there—and not a little guilt. The uneasy solution I have arrived at is to concentrate on teaching during the school year. What research and writing I do then is focused on literature I am discussing in class. Work aimed for publication I confine to summers. I try for an article a year, readied (not necessarily accepted) for publication or presentation. Sometimes I'm lucky. Right now, as I write this, I am on sabbatical in Cambridge, England. What a difference having great chunks of uninterrupted time has made! It has convinced me anew of the value of my continuing to write for publication—not because of what I will contribute to the profession, but because of what it does for me personally and for my teaching. In writing for my peers rather than for nineteen- or twenty-year-olds, I demand more of myself intellectually. In researching my specialty (which I seldom teach), I encounter on the byways of my readings all sorts of ideas applicable to my classes. I re-experience, too, what it is like to be a student: the frustration when an idea is not going anyplace, strategies resorted to for fighting writer's block, the exhilaration of seeing unexpected relationships—useful insights to share with my students next year. Suddenly, too, as a result of research I have done for my sabbatical project, I have begun to see my old lectures in a new way and realize that the basis of my next publication may lie in the material I thought was done just for class preparation. The pressure to publish

will probably always feel like a monkey on my back, but I am not sure I would get rid of it even if I could [Carson].

I do not feel the tension—or at least I did not, back before I became provost and had enough time to "do" scholarship. I wrote because I loved it and because it provided me with a way to put into print what I was saying in class. All my scholarship comes directly from my class preparation, and my classes have been a source of ideas for most of my published work. Early on, I realized that I was not at "the cutting edge" of anything. What I had to say was interesting, but I was not of the first rank of scholars in my field. This did not make me unhappy. I just liked to write, and I liked to see my name in print. I also enjoyed grantsmanship, because I am small-minded enough to like to show the scientists and social scientists that humanists can play the game, too! I still have one more (unimportant) book in me, which will give me enormous satisfaction and will not make a damn to many others. I still love to write [Gittleman].

College professors are a special breed of professionals, at the same time scholars and teachers. I cannot conceive of a professor who can be an outstanding teacher without first having been a student. Likewise, good teachers demand of themselves the production of ideas, concepts, and relationships in the world of research, writing, and grantsmanship. In the first place, teachers tend to teach in the ways they were taught. Poor teachers beget poor teachers, and professors who do not engage in research and writing projects beget students who have little or no interest in scholarly pursuits. In the second place, I object to the word "obligation" in this question. Scholarship, research, and writing are not obligations. They are privileges enjoyed by professors. In what other profession would I have the opportunity, facilities, time, and environment to be at the same time a scholar and a teacher? I am employed at a small, liberal arts, church-affiliated institution. My life is intertwined as a teacher, counselor, leader, administrator, minister, researcher, writer, editor, and officer of professional organizations that formulate policy for the profession. I have piles of manuscripts that I have never submitted for publication. I have files of papers delivered at professional meetings that are not published. All of these have been as important as those papers and books I have published. All have been used in classrooms and laboratories. All serve as examples to students of field research and techniques. Volumes of technical reports I have written as a consultant serve as examples in my classroom. Surely no one has a better life than I [Richason].

Professors were responsible for starting the current trend, in which research and scholarship are normative expectations in our profession. There was a time, after all, when no one expected us to bring in grant dollars or "do" formal "scholarship" aimed at publication. It was not some college president or dean who issued a memorandum ordering that henceforth professors would have to direct part of their efforts away from the classroom and toward our peers at other institutions. No; we started this ourselves, and we did so because it seemed a natural extension of our jobs. We were not content merely to convey knowledge. We also wanted to be discoverers; and having discovered some things, we wanted to share them, not merely with our own students but also with our peers at other institutions, so that they could share them with their students. And then we learned that we could best make certain kinds of discoveries—particularly those in the sciences—if we found external sources of support for the time and the equipment we needed.

Events gradually conspired to cause what was originally merely a diversion—even a luxury—to become an expectation and then even a requirement. If we want to, we can lament the current state of affairs, and many of us do. Surely we are justified in sounding warnings about the state of the profession that has subtly redefined words like "research" and "scholarship" to mean "bringing in lots of grant money" and "publishing lots of pages." Surely we should bring the full weight of our profession to bear against the tendency to redefine "evaluation" as "counting." Surely we must insist on the value of diversity in the professoriate, insist that there is more than one way to show success or progress in a profession as complex as ours. Surely we must insist that it is in the best interests both of professors and of students that reasonable time and support be given to professors who are inclined to do active and contributory scholarship, research, and writing.

Nevertheless, we must not forget that we entered this profession in part because it both permits us and encourages us to be active scholars. It is interesting that not a single one of us CASE finalists feels that we should expect nothing except classroom teaching from members of our profession. If nothing else, we all demand continued learning, the "re-search" that men and women of the mind, true scholars who stay alert and excited and exciting, have always done. For many of us, our own inclinations urge us to participate in a wider arena of teaching than that offered by a roomful of nineteen-year-olds. Perhaps all we need to do, from time to time, is warn those who seem to be in charge of this profession, without being quite in it, that if they work too hard to force all of us to do what most of us want to do anyway, then they may take the fun out of it for everyone. If scholarship, research, and writing become fixed requirements of this noble profession, then the nobility of these activities and of this profession may quietly disappear.

Professors want their students to leave courses more confident, more critical, more knowledgeable, more respectful of ideas, more able to appreciate beauty, more questioning, more powerful, more human, and more capable of passion.

"Students Passionate About Their Learning": The End Products of the Profession

Teaching is a job with so many goals that we professors sometimes lose sight of the main goal . . . whatever that is. Is it our job to teach a body of information? An approach to life? A respect for ideas? A love of truth? An ability to think? An appreciation of beauty? A way to earn a living? We in the profession are in frustrating but glorious confusion about what our primary task is with respect to our students.

The Power of Knowledge

Teaching is like fathering, but my power as a teacher is not based on my students' dependence on me for money or clothes or food or shelter. Rather, it is based on what I know and on what I know how to do. I have knowledge, and that knowledge gives me the only real power I have over students. Yes, I dispense grades, but those are chicken feed, and they give me power only over the chickens. The essential power of the professoriate is the power of knowledge. Students come into my power because I know something they do not know, something they need to know if they want to get along better in the world. I know which books are most worth reading, and why. I know how to write an essay that persuades. I know

P. G. Beidler (ed.). *Distinguished Teachers on Effective Teaching.*
New Directions for Teaching and Learning, no. 28. San Francisco: Jossey-Bass, Winter 1986.

why Chaucer is recognized as the father of English literature. I know how to take twelve little facts and synthesize them into one big opinion. I know why Ahab is a greater man than Starbuck, even though he is less good. I know how to turn words into money. I know why money is infinitely less worth having than either knowledge or the power that comes with it.

I love the power knowledge gives me. I know how uncomfortable and reverential I feel in the presence of people who have more knowledge than I have, and I like knowing that others feel slightly uncomfortable and reverential in my presence. When I discuss two pieces of freshman writing with my freshmen, we generally both know which piece is better. I also have the power of knowing that I can find the words to explain why one theme is better. My freshmen often cannot do that, for they are going by true (but, to them, unexplainable) instinct when they pick one theme over another. I like knowing more than my freshmen do because knowing puts me in control, gives me the power not to sound like a fool when I try to talk about writing.

I love walking into my Chaucer class on the first day, knowing that I am the only one in the room who can read Middle English aloud and understand what it says. I like having the power to know enough about Chaucer to ask the questions. My students do not know that much, and that puts them in a position of powerlessness and dependence.

My job as a teacher is to empower my students, to demystify a subject for them and so give up my power over them. If I am doing my job, by the end of the semester my students are independent of me. I strive every semester to give my students power, even though when I succeed I inevitably disempower myself. I hate that feeling of powerlessness at the end of the semester. And I love it.

My question to the other CASE finalists was:

What is the single most important quality, skill, or attitude you want your students to have after a semester in one of your classes?

There was almost no agreement among the CASE finalists on how to answer this question. Virtually all were uncomfortable with the question. As Ken Eble put it, "I can answer no such question without asking 'When?' or 'In what way?' or 'For how long?' or 'In relation to what?' Today I might want this of my students. And tomorrow? And next year?" Still, almost all the respondents gamely replied, knowing that in the end they would probably be standing alone with their answers.

I Fear a Nation of Sheep

No one else gave quite my answer: "power." Several, however, said something similar by answering "confidence":

I want my students to have confidence in their ability to reason and to argue orally or in writing. There are many other qualities that I would like them to have, but self-reliance is the most important. In addition to knowing how to shape an argument, students should be able to do the research necessary to support the argument and to have the courage to present it. The ability to interpret and to do research is a prerequisite for democracy. What I fear most of all is a nation of sheep—uncritical, unreflective, and obedient. I try as a professor not to develop leaders so much as to develop the critical faculty and the self-confidence so necessary for good citizenship and decent government [Higgs].

What I want most for my students is that they leave with an increased sense of confidence in what they do, coupled with a knowledge of what it takes to be truly professional. I try to locate and highlight their capabilities, as a foundation of confidence upon which they can build [Norris].

Confidence. Not to remember substance as much as to recall method, the way to find out, to solve a problem, to approach a text, to ask better questions, to earn insights, to experience the power and clarity of moments of intuitive awareness [Albertson].

I would like them to feel confident that they could pick up a poem written in English, whether of a previous century or of our own, and read it with understanding and enjoyment. This confidence is, of course, the result of having learned a variety of subskills, which all together make up the skill of "reading a poem." These subskills include sensing the contour of sentences, feeling the cadence and melody of written English, being able to "hear" written English in the ear, being used to the oblique and concise manner of poetic language, sensing the implicit speaker in the poem, interpreting the tonality of the written word, feeling the genre in which the poem is working. Students cannot hope to gain this confidence without having read a lot of poems [Vendler].

We Do Not Want Skilled Barbarians

Others also want a kind of independence for their students, although they approach this goal not so much through students' confidence as through their ability to do the kind of critical thinking or questioning that leads to independence of mind:

I want my students to learn how to think thoroughly, thoughtfully, and critically. I want them to learn how to be honest learners. I want them to learn how and when to be dependent on the professor, and how and when to strike out on their own. All of us are dependent on others throughout our professional lives. We need to appreciate the giants of the past, on whose shoulders we stand. We need to seek the aid of our colleagues. Science has become so specialized and complicated that the team approach to problem solving is almost mandatory. I want my students to learn how to learn from each other. I want my students to learn that the burden of learning is on the learner [Richason].

I want my students to be able to form opinions and make judgments on their own, using only the skills of critical thinking I have taught them. I always tell my students that the conclusions to which they come are of only secondary importance to me. What is primary is that they be able to provide cogent arguments for the positions they take [Ulrich].

After a semester of anthropology, a student should be able to question statements about the concepts in anthropology [Bass].

I want them to learn in the process of responding to literature intellectually and emotionally, to love the question (as Rilke said), knowing that if we take joy in asking questions, it is just possible that one day something like an answer may appear [Carson].

I want students to be able to formulate problems and think about them from various viewpoints. I want them to appreciate that they cannot solve problems unless they marshall facts, sift through data, and establish a framework for solving them. But I also want students to incorporate compassion and values into the solution of a problem. Example: "Here are four alternate solutions to the world food problem. How do your personal values influence your thinking when we consider the cost-effectiveness of each solution?" [Sisler].

Most of all, I want my students, after having been through a semester in one of my classes, to be able to formulate questions a bit more on their own than they could when they first entered my class, questions couched in slightly broader terms than those they would have used before [Aveni].

I hope my course will help produce a person who has acquired a knowledge of analytical concepts and who can think straight, communicate ideas, evaluate conditions, and discriminate between the important and the unimportant. We do not want skilled barbarians; we want graduates who have technical skills but who know what to do with these skills [Ratliff].

The Life of the Mind Forever

For some professors, the primary purpose of college teaching is to put students in touch with ideas, knowledge, truth:

I want my students to have a proper respect for ideas—their own ideas and the ideas of others. I cannot claim that my students develop that respect in all my courses, but there is one in which we move toward the ideal. In a summer program that I offer with a colleague, we examine social and environmental issues in two regions: northern New York and Appalachia. Our role as instructors consists largely of putting students in direct proximity with the ideas of others. When we consider strip mining in Appalachia, for example, the students talk with strip miners, mine operators, environmental activists, government regulators, and local citizens. My students' own ideas undergo real change, and it becomes very difficult for them to cherish, let alone advance, an unexamined idea again [Marden].

I want them to develop curiosity, to want to know. I want them to be able to apply what they know to real situations and to do so with proper respect for truth [Hofman].

The attitude that I hope my students will take away with them is that it is important to know, to be aware of the world and how it works. This is important, not merely because it will make their lives more interesting, but also because it is a *duty* incumbent upon all of us to participate actively in creating a better future world [Clark].

How do I express the idea of "getting the candle lit"? My goal is to make college the preparatory time for lifelong learning, to make people feel that they have become intellectuals who are turned on to the life of the mind forever [Gittleman].

A Single Flower of the Horse Chestnut Tree

Poetic idealism lurks not far beneath the surface of most good teachers:

> I hope my students will be more human. I would like to think that in my courses some students develop a view of life that can accommodate loss and suffering, an awareness that love almost always calls for self-sacrifice, an ability to be joyfully surprised by a single flower of the horse chestnut tree, a reverence for words [Eichner].

> I want students after one of my courses to "see feelingly" (to borrow Shakespeare's phrase). The "seeing" requires active intellectual perception and refinement. The "feeling" requires an equally demanding amount of passion. To feel, we must allow sympathy and empathy to inspire learning, we must listen intensely, and we must subordinate the self to stand under the idea or situation with respect, with humility, and with awe. Because I teach literature, I want my students to love literature—to laugh, cry, feel about it. Because I love literature myself, I want my students to read well enough to encounter literary pieces accurately, so that their laughter or tears will be appropriate responses to the works of art they are interpreting, rather than to "interpretations" that have little basis beyond their own fictionalizing. Ultimately, I hope that what my students see feelingly in literature will translate into a richer experience of life as they live it and as they continue to experience it through art [Empric].

> My students must have a body of knowledge about what is known and what is not known in the particular course that I teach. They must have the ability to take that knowledge and use it to address fundamental questions they have not seen before. They must have the skills to read, to understand, and to communicate in written language the insights and knowledge that they have. But, above all, I want my students to be passionate about their learning, to feel an existential joy and pleasure in it [Saltman].

In the end, we want our students to have it all—the knowledge, the words, the confidence, the humanity, the wisdom, the passion, the power, the joy, the thinking, the ideas, the beauty, the reverence. We can never give it all to any one student; but, year after year, we hold on to our ambition and our optimism.

*Students learn best in many ways, depending on who they are,
what they are studying, and who is teaching them. They learn
by doing, by observing, by discussing, by experiencing, by
having examples, and by connecting with the minds and
spirits of professors.*

"As Long as There Is Personal Engagement": The Way Students Learn

Teaching is a complex art, if only because there is no teaching unless
those being taught actually learn. And learning is an even more complex
art than teaching. We professors do our thing before students (lecturing),
beside students (showing), or behind students (pushing), but in the end it
is they who either learn or fail to learn. None of us has a magic formula
about how students learn, but most of us are able to isolate a thing or two
about how some students learn best from us.

Do It Yourself, Johnny

I generally learn best and most permanently by doing something.
It is useful in some ways to have others tell me what to do or show me
how to do it, but it is still theirs when they are finished; it is mine only
when I have done it myself.

In my classes, then, I almost never lecture. When I do, I never lecture for more than fifteen minutes. I am not much good at lecturing anyway, and so no one is missing much when I refrain from doing it. I
suppose I could learn to be better at it by doing more of it, but my heart

P. G. Beidler (ed.). *Distinguished Teachers on Effective Teaching.*
New Directions for Teaching and Learning, no. 28. San Francisco: Jossey-Bass, Winter 1986.

would never be in it. There are better ways for students to learn what I have to teach.

I do not have a body of information to convey. Rather, as a professor of English, I teach technique and seeing and criticism and writing and self-awareness and how to ask questions and, occasionally, honesty and virtue and truth and beauty. I used to try to lecture about such subjects, but I have come to see that my students will learn what I have to teach not by telling but by their doing. It was doing that convinced me. Gradually, slowly, sometimes painfully, I have come to understand that only doing will convince my students.

In my classes, then, I try to get my students doing something whenever I can. In a recent sophomore survey of American literature, for example, I gave daily quizzes at the start of class on material assigned for that class. Once my students had taken the daily quiz on, say, the first quarter of *Moby-Dick*, they knew that they would never have to answer a for-credit question on that material again, because I had promised not to give either hourly exams or a final. After the quiz on the first quarter of *Moby-Dick* was over, my students knew that they did not have to listen to my opinions or ever prove that they had listened to my opinions by writing them back to me on an exam. I used this rather unconventional teaching technique because I wanted my students to do that enormous book for themselves, not to hear about my experience of Ahab.

Before each quiz, I gave my students an opportunity to ask me (or their fellow classmates) any questions they wanted to ask. I encouraged them to try to anticipate my quiz questions, and I promised that if they happened to ask a question that would appear on the quiz, I would give them my answer or (more likely, unless it was a "fact" question) give them a chance to discuss it among themselves under my leadership. In the first classes of the course, my students asked few questions. Toward the end, however, they were asking many questions, and I found myself giving the daily quiz closer and closer to the end of the period.

By the end of the semester, my course was no long really "mine" because the students were doing more of the questions and answers—that is, the essential teaching—than I was. I always directed the discussion, and I am skilled at bending or twisting or rephrasing both questions and answers from students so that the points I think are most important get made. But that course was memorable for almost all of us because I did so little of the "doing." It was not an easy way to teach, because I had to be ready to answer questions and at times to slide questions around to other questions I thought were more important. But for me, it was a good way because those students were reading literature as if their lives depended on it. They knew I would have no answers for them before the quiz unless they learned to read thoroughly and carefully and to ask good questions.

I have my students "doing" as much as possible in my basic composition classes, too. A couple of years ago, for example, I decided that instead of having my freshmen read one of the hundreds of textbooks on writing, I would have them collectively write their own. I have noticed during some twenty years of teaching freshman composition that students can tell good writing from bad writing. That is, if I mimeographed three themes written by my students and then had them vote on which was best, their assessment almost always agreed with mine. I decided that in their almost intuitive ability to distinguish good writing from bad, there was something to build a course on.

On the second day of that class, before I had said a word about what I "looked for" in good writing, I had my students each write an in-class essay on "The Loneliness of the Lehigh Freshman." I told them I would not grade their essays, but I wanted them to do the best writing they could. Then I selected—more or less at random—six of their essays and duplicated them. I gave them to the students at the next class period. I asked the students to read the six themes quickly and rank-order them from one to six, according to whatever principles of good writing they wanted to apply. They wrote their rankings on a slip of paper and we did a quick tally on the board. Having thus identified the theme with the highest ranking, I then asked the students to reread it and tell me why they liked it better than the five that got fewer votes. Every time someone said something that others in the class seemed to agree with, I had the class stenographer write it down. That day we ended with the beginnings of a rough list of principles of good writing: "use of examples"; "makes a single point"; "supports the main point"; "orderly movement from beginning to end"; "writer seems to be in control"; "interesting introduction." In the next several weeks, we expanded and refined the list and added examples for each principle. By mid-semester, we had a twelve-page booklet on the principles of good writing.

In the last four themes of the semester, I began grading their writing according to the principles outlined in our booklet. That part was easy, because the list we had arrived at in our discussions was a good list, almost exactly the list I would have come up with on my own. To be sure, I had directed the discussion somewhat, had encouraged some avenues of discussion and quietly discouraged or ignored certain others, but in the end the list of principles was the students' own, and I was able to say— and mean—that I would give them all A's on their paper unless I could show specifically that they had violated one or more of the principles in our booklet. The grading process was more successful than before, in part because those freshmen, in writing the criteria themselves, had "bought into" them. These were not principles of good writing that came down from on high in some "egghead" lecture or from some principle maker in the sky. These were their own principles, principles they at least half-understood because they had discovered and articulated them themselves.

They knew what I meant when I said their themes lacked unity, because they had told me that they liked themes with unity better than ones that made no single point. They knew that they had to use examples, because they had told me that they preferred concrete writing to abstract writing. The grading that semester went better because the learning had gone better, and the learning had gone better because my students taught themselves. They had done the doing.

Had other teachers, I wondered, discovered as I had that students learn best by doing? I tried to find out by asking the CASE finalists this question:

> **What, in your opinion, is the most important way students learn? By example? By reading? By practical assignments? By discussion?**

There was little agreement on how to answer this question. Some CASE finalists all but refused to answer, on the basis that students learn in an enormous number of ways. Still, most of them attempted to share their thoughts and experiences about what was most important and, in doing so, said some things worth repeating here. Virtually all of them prefaced the paragraphs I quote below with some general statement, such as "There are almost as many ways to learn as there are students." I generally have eliminated such statements and gone directly to their attempts to focus on "the" or "a" most important way students learn.

Six Egg Yolks and Salt Shakers

Three people—interestingly, but not surprisingly, all teachers of some form of science—found, as I had, that learning by doing is important:

> One of the most effective ways to learn is by doing. As a teacher of astronomy, especially ancient astronomy, I try to involve my students in my work. We have an observatory here at the university. I demand that my students visit the observatory at least six times during the term if they want to pass my astronomy courses. They must look through the telescopes, draw sketches, take notes, keep a journal. Why? Because I believe that my students can learn about the sky only by confronting it directly, by watching the stars and planets move, by recording their positions. We can read all we care to in books about how the marvelous heavenly drama unfolds, but the only way to comprehend it is to see it acted out for ourselves. Then, during our one-month January term, I take students to Mexico, where we work in the field together. We study Maya inscriptions and we measure

the plans and orientations of pyramids. We do fieldwork in archeoastronomy, based on the readings we did in class the previous fall term. The students who come with me on those field trips learn not only more about the workings of the ancient Native American mind but also more about me. In the field we live together, we eat together, we talk and walk together. We confront one another in a different way than in the classroom, where I am in a somewhat adversarial position, behind the desk, with them "on the other side" taking notes. So, for me, fieldwork—in the observatory or on-site among the ancient Mexican ruins—is the best way I can help my students to learn by doing [Aveni].

The most important way students learn is by being involved in research projects. In a laboratory science, they learn more by being in the lab and working with junior and senior or graduate-level students, as well as with faculty. They learn equipment techniques and are in a position to listen to discussions about a particular field and its problems [Bass].

In biology, the greatest learning goes on when students physically contact their subject matter in the laboratory or in the field. Unfortunately, current budget constraints make such direct experience less and less available. And here, I would warn teachers against trying to introduce electronic substitutes. Videofilms are, in my opinion, largely a waste of time. The teaching level is usually poor, and students do what they always do when watching TV: They stop thinking. Far better to lecture, to pass around real objects, and to carry out classroom demonstrations. Almost every lecture, I bring in something to demonstrate a point. Protein denaturation is a class experiment, with six egg yolks, six forks, and six salt shakers. Each student shakes salt on the yolks, stirs it, and passes it to the next one. In five minutes, two-hundred students have participated, and all the yolks are hard as cement. No one forgets [Clark].

As Provincial As It Sounds

Some professors are bold enough to defend lecturing as an effective way to teach:

As provincial and self-serving as it sounds, I feel that students learn best from carefully prepared and well-delivered lectures. Many of us teach in disciplines that are continually changing. The body of literature is immense, and ideas are always being challenged. I believe that a university professor has the obligation to draw from this churning cauldron the most important data and concepts. We must synthesize them, present the various arguments and countervailing views. As a teacher with this philosophy, I must be direct and candid in telling the students what I am doing, and that the views I express are my own interpretations. Readings and assignments, of course, are important, and discussions add breadth and allow the students to challenge my interpretations, but the lecture is the focal point of my teaching [Sisler].

My courses are pretty traditional, large lectures on general humanities subjects, with no prerequisites. I am not an innovative teacher. I give two open-book, take-home exams because I want to find out what they know, not what they don't know. The reading is very important, but my lectures are also important, and class participation—although I am talking about classes with three hundred and four hundred students—is considerable. I do lecture, but every class, I throw out about ten questions with the intent of provoking. In my classes, students seem to get the most out of the material when I succeed in getting them to think about their own place in the scheme of things. I love to take them back, to place them in a historical context, to make them feel that it is important to understand their place in this grand scheme. I love to light the candle. When I do, then everything comes together: the tests, the reading, the lectures, even the out-of-class discussions [Gittleman].

A Payoff in Pleasure

Theories of teaching are as mysterious as theories of learning. Many good teachers appear to stop worrying about the theories and just walk into the classroom and try something that seems to have worked in the past or seems as if it may work this time with these students. Asking some teachers how students learn almost seems to be the wrong question. Some of us are not sure how students learn. We just walk in and make it all happen.

Students learn by measuring their ideas against those of others. As a consequence, the effective teacher starts by recognizing that students already know a good deal and simply provides a good yardstick and some things to measure—good books, the skeleton of a fish, a work of art, a social policy [Marden].

How do students learn? How does anyone learn? Present-day theorists are ingenious in showing developmental patterns in learning. They attract some teachers to searching for the right theory upon which their teaching can be built. But just as I think most human learning is experiential, so do I learn most of what I use in teaching through active experience. I respect what careful study has revealed about how people learn, but I am as much attracted by the mysteries of learning. Why do I, and my students, remember what we do remember? Why, for example, should I have learned so many popular songs, and why should one come into my head, quite without bidding and letter-perfect, forty years after I last heard it? Still, mysteries cannot remain complete mysteries when one is exposed to them year after year in individual after individual, and so there are some things about learning that seem no less mysterious for being basic. I would say that an important basic point is that we learn largely what we want to learn. Learning, as both Plato and Aristotle argued, is man's greatest pleasure, even though that statement may seem to be in conflict with our own memories of grueling, hard study to accomplish some difficult learning. Still, all learning begins with a desire to learn and has a payoff in pleasure. The pleasure for certain kinds of learning may be deferred, and surely the pleasure is various in its manifestations. Put in the context of teaching, then, arousing activity and assisting the student in finding pleasure in that activity are central. Teaching and learning must be active. We do most things because we want to, and finding ways of making students want to is what I search for. The point may be that learning is such a great human urge and affords such pleasure that we need to do little more than open doors and not stand in the way. Most of my teaching aims at enlarging the pleasures that can come from learning and at showing ways to gain access to those pleasures. A good part of that is my manifesting my own delight in learning and encouraging students to manifest theirs [Eble].

Reading, Writing, and Asking

A number of CASE finalists emphasized the importance of two closely related ways of learning: reading and writing. Reading, of course, is a tried and true method of learning, and it is clear that one of the primary functions of any teacher is to direct students to the right books. As for writing, it is easy to think of writing as merely reporting what one has already learned, but everyone who has done much writing is aware that writing is the process of learning, of discovering, what it is we know. Many professors discover that to ask questions is often an effective way to encourage students to focus both their reading and their writing.

> Writing is an important feature of learning. I learn more when the reins of the process are in my own hands, when I am discovering rather than repeating. I see students learning most when they are active rather than passive, permitted to learn from their own mistakes rather than profiting from mine, choosing freely for themselves rather than performing within prescribed limitations [Albertson].

> Observation and measurement may be the best way to knowledge of the world *(scientia)*, but writing is the best way to self-knowledge *(gnosis)*. I believe Alice in Wonderland was essentially right when she said, "How can I know what I think until I see what I say?" We learn about the experience of others by reading, but we best learn about ourselves by writing. I do not see how we can get very far in the humanities without asking for a lot of reading and writing [Higgs].

> Students learn best by actively seeking answers to questions. If my enthusiasm for the subject arouses their curiosity so that they search for answers and get into the habit of reading, I think I am being helpful to them in their education [Ratliff].

> Students learn best when they prepare themselves to answer pertinent questions. The focal point of my course is the weekly quiz, in which I ask the students the questions they must be able to answer if they have indeed mastered the material [Hofman].

> I do not think it is possible to learn without reading. It consolidates what one hears in lecture, and many people take in material better through the eyes than through the ears. Studying is better done when it is focused by practical assignments. I find that students "get more" out of a poem when they are asked to think about several questions while they read it, in preparation for discussion in section meeting [Vendler].

For years, I thought there was only one way of learning. That it happened to be precisely the way I learn best never struck me as odd. I catch on easily by reading and by imitation through writing. While not particularly creative, I am good at analysis, at seeing central ideas, identifying supporting specifics, and synthesizing what I have just learned with old knowledge. Expecting my students to do the same, I constructed writing assignments and examinations requiring these skills. Now I know that there are a number of different kinds of learners—from the linear learner, who needs step-by-step practical guidance, to the global learner, who seems capable of skipping all the intermediate stages and with dazzling (and, to us more orderly folk, sometimes messy) creativity arriving at a new idea. This recognition of diversity made me rethink many of my writing assignments. I now try to provide choices, enabling students to learn and to express ideas in a variety of ways. So, while I require all my American literature students to write an original critical analysis of some work, I now give them options. The global learners can discover and display their knowledge of Poe by writing a short story imitating him, while the more linear learner may begin by summarizing and evaluating major critical articles on "The Fall of the House of Usher." I also try to recognize different learning styles in exams, combining long essays requiring synthesis or original insights with shorter, one-paragraph responses based on more specific knowledge of the works studied [Carson].

Seduction by Example

A surprising number of CASE finalists decided that one of the most important ways students learned is by example. Yet this should not be surprising, because we as teachers are also learners, and part of our job is to show by our own examples how much fun and profit we derive from learning:

> When I realize how much I have learned by listening to and watching teachers, scientists, philosophers, poets, and others, I realize once again that example is "the way" [Eichner].

> Students learn best by example. It is in the observation of the skillful performance of a master and his or her dedication to excellence that students are best nurtured. The teacher-student relationship is much like a master-apprentice relationship [Ulrich].

My challenge is intellectually and emotionally to seduce each student in my class to the subject that I teach. I do so by personal example. I am passionate about every course I teach. I am as passionate about biology for nonmajors in a "Food and Nutrition" course for four hundred skeptics as I am for my one-to-one interactions with graduate students in the laboratory [Saltman].

If I had to choose the most important way students learn, I would be forced to conclude from experience that it is by example. I wanted to learn, wanted to research, wanted to write, wanted to publish, wanted to be an excellent teacher because of the examples I observed in my own student days. Now, I try to set an example for my students to follow. When I was a young professor, I tried to show students what they could do as young people. Today, my role is one of a professional father [Richason].

Building Bridges to Students

I shall close with two statements, both emphasizing in different ways the importance of the professor's personal involvement in the learning process of students:

Learning happens in a variety of ways for each individual. In fact, learning is stimulated by the very variety of the ways, as long as there is the essential component of personal engagement. Learning is also somewhat at the mercy of circumstance. A personal experience can cause a student to learn at a level very different from the norm expected of undergraduates. Tolstoy's "The Death of Ivan Illyich" will not merely lie on the page for someone with a family member dying in the hospital. I recall one undergraduate lecture on *King Lear,* during which a popular and dynamic professor stopped reading portions of a final scene and stood in front of a class of men while tears streamed down his face. He excused himself from the class, and while no one asked and he never ventured an explanation, that is one scene in literature whose power no one in that class will ever question or forget. It is important for a teacher to recognize which techniques work best for him or her and to rely on those most often. Beyond this, though, the incorporation of a variety of learning experiences seems to be the best way to ensure personally engaging many of the one's students most of the time [Empric].

How best does a student learn? A student learns best when somehow a teacher finds a way to establish an intellectual bond with him or her. When two minds are caused to meet, then all flows from that bonding. That bond can develop in different ways, depending on the teacher, the student, and the circumstances. I try to form that bond whenever I can. When I meet a student, I look for positive things, little hints of a deeper capability. It may be facility with language. It may be the seeing eye of curiosity. It may be a sunny spirit. I discover such things during walks together, as we wonder why mesquite roots wander so far, or when we seek shelter at noon under the arroyo bank and talk of our friends or aspirations, or when I read the journal or notebook of a student too shy to talk with me face to face. Then I try to begin the process of unfolding that will convince the student of his or her worth, and I suggest some way the student might use his or her special talent. Bridges to students come in no single way. They come from everything the student is and does, meeting everything the professor is and does [Norris].

There is no one most important way that students learn, although it well may be that for each student there is at any one moment one best way. Our job as professors is to discover the one best way for as many of our individual students as we can. For most of our students, we shall not fully succeed. For some, we shall fail miserably. For most of those few for whom we succeed most fully, we shall never know that we have succeeded, because students are embarrassed to tell us such things. Sometimes we find out, however, and when we do, finding out makes up for all the times when we cannot be sure. Helping a student find the best way to learn is sometimes called love.

Good teachers are not bored with their work. They find ways— through the subjects they teach, the courses they teach, the students they teach, or their own enlivening personalities— to avoid boredom.

"A Wise but Lonely Wanderer": How Professors Avoid Getting Bored— and Boring

Good teaching is stimulating. That little sentence has a double meaning, and both parts are true: good teaching causes us professors to be stimulated, and good teaching causes us to stimulate others. Although we tend to teach the same courses year after year to students who, at least in the aggregate, vary little from one year to the next, the best among us find ways to keep from getting bored with the assembly-line aspects of education.

Bright, Curious, and Articulate

Professors are a curious breed. We are bright, or at least smart enough to have done well in most of the courses we took in college and in graduate school. We are curious. We enjoy discovering new things, bumping into new ideas, exploring new worlds, delving to new depths, soaring to new heights. And we are articulate. We love to use the spoken and the written word. We know that words have a power that neither love nor

P. G. Beidler (ed.). *Distinguished Teachers on Effective Teaching.*
New Directions for Teaching and Learning, no. 28. San Francisco: Jossey-Bass, Winter 1986.

money has, and we revel in using the power of words to good effect. If we were not bright, curious, and articulate, we would not be professors.

And what do we bright, curious, and articulate professors do with our lives? We spend them in classrooms, teaching basically the same subjects to basically the same students, year after year. As we get older and wiser, our students seem to get not only younger but also a shade less bright, curious, and articulate. As we grow more advanced in our subjects, however, most of us still have to teach at the introductory level each year.

How do we bright, curious, and articulate professors avoid boredom? I can speak only for myself. I must confess, first of all, that I do not entirely avoid it. But because I know that when I am bored I am also boring, I seek desperately to avoid the boredom that seemed to cripple so many of the teachers I have had through the years. Boredom is the cancer of our profession.

I have a number of different antiboredom strategies. One is to publish, to challenge myself to say in black words on white pages a few things never said before. Publishing is teaching, of course, and much of what I publish is boring, but at least I have no captive audience when I publish, nobody who is forced to read my words. Another strategy is to take creative sabbaticals. Sabbaticals seem to come along at just about the time when I think I cannot face another story or book or poem or student. Still another strategy—my personal favorite—is to find a particular student to connect with each semester. This student rises out of the aggregate with a face that does not go away at the end of the class or the end of the semester and reminds me by his or her presence in my office or over coffee in the snack bar that there are real souls to be moved through teaching. My most effective way to avoid boredom in this profession, however, is to teach new courses. Teaching new courses allows me to feel that I am challenging my brightness, satisfying my curiosity, and using my powers of articulation in fresh ways.

I can best illustrate how teaching new courses helps me to avoid boredom by describing my first course on the American Indian. A dozen years ago, I was bored with my usual course fare and decided to offer a seminar I called "The Indian in America." I knew very little about American Indians. I had never studied Indians in any course at any level anywhere. My field, after all, was English. Indians were not an important subject in British literature and were unfortunately all but ignored as subjects of American literature. I knew that I had no training in Indian studies, but I was arrogant enough to think that I was bright, I was curious about Indians, and I knew that after reading some books I could become articulate. I looked through some catalogues, ordered ten books for the course, and waited to see if any students would show up. They did. On the first day of class, I explained that I knew almost nothing about Indians, but I was curious and wanted to learn by reading and discussing some interesting-looking books. If the students wanted to join me, I said, I would be pleased to have them come along. If they did not, I would be happy to help them pick a course that was more to their liking, either in my department or in some other, a course in which the professor knew something about the subject. They all elected to stay in my course and learn with me about Indians.

That was a wonderful course, that first course on American Indians. I was not a bit bored, and neither were my students. Through that course, we all began to satisfy our curiosity about Indians and gradually grew articulate about them. I, for one, became sufficiently articulate about Indians that the following year I was able to write a successful application to the National Endowment for the Humanities for a postdoctoral fellowship in the anthropology department at the University of Arizona to study about Indians in a more formal way. After that year, and after teaching two more new courses about Indians and the literature written about them and by them, I became sufficiently articulate to write two books and a dozen articles about Indians. Not all attempts to avoid boredom result in such a pedigree, of course, but the point stands: By teaching new courses, or new twists on old courses, I am usually able to be simultaneously stimulated and stimulating.

I wondered how my fellow CASE finalists managed to keep their teaching stimulating. My question to them was this:

> **How do you, who teach essentially the same subject matter to essentially the same kinds of students year after year, keep from being bored and boring as a teacher? How do you, as you get older, maintain the enthusiasm you had when you entered the profession?**

I got fine answers to this question. Some CASE finalists emphasized, as I have done, the stimulation of the courses they teach. Others had more to say about their fascination with their research subjects. Others talked about the stimulation students provided them. Still others suggested that their own personalities provided sufficient pedagogical jolt. All in all, it appears that in one way or another, award-winning teachers have found ways to be neither bored nor boring. In most of the selections I present here, I have tried to focus on the central point that each CASE finalist made, although many of them also mentioned a number of other ways they avoid being bored and boring.

Freshmen Are Exciting People

For many professors, the students themselves are an almost endless source of stimulation:

I see this as perhaps the biggest challenge facing the teacher—how to stay alive intellectually, especially in the classroom. I do not believe there are any simple solutions to this problem, but the best way I have found to deal with it is to keep the focus upon the students as much as possible, rather than on the material taught. As a teacher, I try to assist the students on their route to self-knowledge. They are there to learn about themselves; Jonathan Edwards, Benjamin Franklin, Nathaniel Hawthorne, and Walt Whitman just happened to be individuals whose works can shed light upon their knowledge of themselves. After all, neither literature nor science is to be revered; both are to be enjoyed, and we enjoy them most when we see them as means to self-knowledge, rather than as ends in themselves. Often we tend to think of literature as a display of precious jewels under guard and glass, which we as weary curators must show year in and year out to unappreciative peasants who have been required to march by us. I prefer another image, that of the teacher as a wise but lonely wanderer, a kind of singing peddler, who comes upon a group of innocent and ignorant youngsters and convinces them that the sparkling rocks he carries in his old buckets can enlighten their lives if they will take them out of the buckets, handle them, share them, turn them over and over to see how they catch the light [Higgs].

I teach chemistry to students. I have made it a point to know the students to whom I teach chemistry. Three years ago, I had Karen Povinelli and Ron Knipe in my course. Two years ago, it was Jane Bailey and John Zic. Last year, it was Nina Mutone and Chris Lucey. This year, it is Jill Gordon and Pat Cooke. There is no way that I can know Karen, Ron, Jane, John, Nina, Chris, Jill, and Pat and be bored. Freshmen are exciting people. They have an independence they have never had before, and they do not yet have the responsibilities they are going to have. They are really beginning their travels in life. They need so much help. Realizing how fragile they are in that crucial stage of life and how much potential they have is the inspiration that makes me want to do the best job I can. They deserve no less [Hofman].

It is easy to stay enthusiastic teaching biology to nonmajors each year. The reason is simply that my reward is the students' enthusiasm. Each pair of bright eyes, each puzzled expression, each inquisitive question after lecture makes being energetic and innovative a natural response. In upper-division courses, I am less successful in this respect. Here, it seems, the students are bored even before they take the classes I teach. Most of them are premedical students nowadays; gone are those who studied biology for the sheer love of the subject. So, clearly, I shall have to find some new approaches to teaching nonmammalian physiology that will intrigue this new clientele [Clark].

The course title may be the same, and the course outline may be the same, but the students are always different. Each successive group of thirty students taking a course is different from all the others, and so the course is never the same [Ratliff].

My Excitement Seems Only to Grow

Several of the CASE finalists were troubled that I even asked the question, because boredom is something they simply do not associate with this profession of ours:

The fact that this question was asked amazes and bothers me. My classroom work is not "business as usual." It is not doing the same old thing at the same old stand on the same old side of the street. I do not teach the same old subject matter to the same old kinds of students. As I reflect on thirty-six years of teaching undergraduate college students, I do not recall ever being bored. If I had, I would have quit the second time around. Each new semester has its own challenges, new materials, different faces, and above all different minds. Each new semester presents itself to me as one in which I am beginning to mold a new mind. Each class presents new problems I have to solve. There is an air of excitement about walking into a classroom. I can hardly wait to discuss with my classes the new things I am doing in the field, at the computer terminal, in the library, or with the map collection. There is nothing boring about my job [Richason].

College teachers have the best life imaginable. We have the necessary ingredient for remaining ever young, and that is the challenge of young minds. It is important that I remain open to the fact that no matter how many times I have been over the material, this is the first time for the students. I am also stimulated by my clinical work as a bioethicist. I do not merely teach bioethics in a classroom; I also work in hospitals and with doctors as an ethics consultant. I work with patients as a counselor, to help them cope with disease and to help them process some of the terrifying decisions that confront them as a result of disease. Every clinical situation is peculiar, and this keeps me always fresh in understanding and applying moral principles. I can then take this freshness into the classroom. Because I do not find my life boring, my students seldom find my courses boring [Ulrich].

I have been scared, exhilarated, outraged, humbled, illumined. I have not been bored [Eichner].

For the naturalist, boredom in teaching is not a problem. I always see new things, discovered right alongside the students. Let me give an example. For years I had marveled at the beauty and symmetry of what we came to call "lupine sapphires," the shining droplets of water caught in the center of the lupine's ring of radial leaflets. The spaces between leaflet margins create stripes of light, making the droplet look like a star sapphire. Was it just chance that these lovely gems were created, or did the lupine bush somehow use them? One day, my students and I set out to unravel the mystery. In the morning, the banks of lupines beside a gravel road were shining with sapphires. Later in the day, there were fewer. And, finally, by dusk they were all gone. The next day, we borrowed a syringe from a first-aid kit, measured the droplets, put them back, and then cut off some leaflets from a plant. In these, we placed identical-sized gems. We watched and measured again. The gems on the cut leaves were soon a third the size of the uncut ones. When they disappeared, the cut leaflets began to droop "Could these leaves drink?" we asked. One student said, "They shouldn't do that. Water only comes in through the roots." Well, to make a long and fascinating odyssey of discovery short, lupines do drink from their leaves. Little sapphires placed on those droopy leaves soon had them nicely erect again. And we made other discoveries, too, such as how the little hairs at the center of the leaflet caught drops that rolled down the leaflet, while other little hairs held them up. None of those students will ever look at a lupine in the old way again, nor will I. As I get older, my excitement with the world and its wonders seems only to grow [Norris].

I Make Interesting Mistakes

Professors who do a lot of lecturing work hard to keep their lectures spontaneous, to avoid repeating their lectures from the previous year:

> I use one trick to remain spontaneous, excited, and a bit frightened when I approach the lecture. I never have a piece of paper or a note on the lectern. I never have a key word on the board. I typically prepare the next day's lectures between eight and eleven in the evening before. During the preparation, I type up notes, draw diagrams, synthesize relevant literature, and consider examples from current events. The morning of the lecture, I write three to six key thoughts on a five-by-eight card. I reserve the last fifteen minutes before the lecture to look at this card and think. I would be terrified if I ever confronted a podium with notes. I blow a concept now and then; I make interesting mistakes, but they do not result from my being ill prepared or complacent. They result from my striving to take that material and spontaneously think and talk it through with a supercritical audience. If I make a mistake, I pick it up next time with a comment like "The part of yesterday's lecture relating to marginal analysis and profit-point determination was completely incomprehensible. Let's have at it again and see if we can get you and me both straightened out" [Sisler].

> I lecture not from notes but only from an outline. I encourage students to ask questions and, to a certain extent, I allow students to lead me in the subject that we discuss in class. I have found as the years go by that attitudes and interests of the students change, and I try to keep abreast of these changes by following a basic outline, but not necessarily teaching exactly the same thing each quarter [Bass].

I Die a Few Times Each Month

Some professors stay fresh by teaching new courses or, more frequently, altering old ones so that they become new:

> To keep from being bored, I change the texts, the syllabus, the visual aids. I try to make the course new enough to be interesting, challenging. I die a few times each month and am forced to prepare, to rewrite, to read again. And the students change. I have to force myself to listen to them, to find out what they

are thinking, singing, longing for. It is so easy to become out of touch, obsolete, a vestigial remnant of the forties, sixties, Vietnam, graduate school, yesterday [Albertson].

I try not to teach the same courses every year. I try to develop new courses as I go along. I also do a lot of team teaching. For example, I taught a course on evolution three years ago with a biologist and a historian. The three of us divided the lectures and discussions, and we all centered on the theme of evolution, as perceived from our respective disciplines. I dealt with the evolutionary theory of the origin of the universe. My biological colleague dealt with the biological theory of evolution, as conceived by Darwin. The historian dealt with social evolution and the attempt nineteenth-century thinkers made to apply Darwin's ideas outside the scientific realm. We all thought it was a genuine thrill to be in class at the same time and to critically examine each other's perspectives [Aveni].

I believe in teaching a variety of classes and have done so throughout my career. I find it a good way to keep out of ruts. In teaching a history-of-ideas course almost every year for thirty years, I do not get bored, because the material has not become an object of academic specialization for me, such that my specialized inquiries become of great interest to me but leave the student behind. Knowing too much is as sure a way to be boring as any. I also with some frequency teach a course called "Introduction to Literature." This course remains fresh because it always exposes students to poems and plays and stories we can get excited about; hence we are not bored. Since there are so many of these, I can always find ones I have not encountered or turn back to ones I have not read lately. In the end, it is the variety of human life—in the students, in the literature, in myself—that is my subject. One of the advantages we older teachers have is that we can be much freer than younger ones. We can be more ourselves and have more self that is of interest to students [Eble].

I Am Always Writing a Book

A professor's subject can often be a source of continuing enthusiasm:

I teach poetry. Poetry has existed as long as written language itself, and no doubt longer. It exists in all languages and has persisted through all cultural vicissitudes. It is still being practiced throughout the world today. It is therefore inexhaustible. My way of understanding poetry is to try to understand the poets one by one. Each one takes about ten years—that means reading the poet until one knows all the poems more or less by heart, knows all their interrelations, has read everything else the poet has written, knows the poetry of his century, and knows the criticism of that poetry (as well as any essential ancillaries, for example, Christianity and its texts to write about George Herbert, or Irish history to write about Yeats). Since I am always writing a book, I am always trying to know some part of poetry intimately in this way. I usually then give a course in that poet (I have given single-author courses in Shakespeare's sonnets, Whitman, Yeats, Stevens, Keats, Lowell, and others). I also do a lot of reviewing of contemporary poetry. This makes me think about new possibilities in the genre and rethink old ones. Also, as one grows older, new poems come into view in older authors. The Yeats poems I most like now are not necessarily the ones that meant the most to me in my twenties and so the emphasis in a course changes over the years. I can always say new things [Vendler].

Every year I seek to learn more about those subjects I am asked to teach. I bring into the classroom the very frontiers of these subjects. Recently I taught a course in advanced nutrition. It was a far cry from examining the four basic food groups and memorizing the names and numbers of the essential amino acids, vitamins, and trace elements. As an experiment, I assigned each student approximately ten pages in a dreadful book called *Life Extension,* by Dirk Pearson and Sandy Shaw. This is a best-selling nutrition book that promises everlasting life and great sex and health. Each student was asked to analyze those ten pages and separate out what was real, what was surreal, and what was unreal. It was a great learning experience for all of us. The most fascinating aspect was that some students were so angry they demanded that the book be banned. When asked about the First Amendment, they admitted they had never really thought about that. Then we discussed how we could educate the public so that it would not be defrauded by such false prophets, and whether and how the government should intervene to help people understand the nature of their biological lives. I guess part of what keeps me enthusiastic is that same strange tension and excitement I have been feeling

ever since I was five years old, when August became Sep-
tember and it was time to go off to school again. Whether I
was carrying a lunch pail, a slide rule, or my lecture notes,
it was as if it were a period of self-renewal and growth, with
new adventures to be enjoyed [Saltman].

The kinds of things that I teach keep me from being bored.
For example, I teach the sociology of medical and health
care. These are exciting times, with changes in the medical
technology, new issues in health-care financing, the emer-
gence of for-profit medical centers, and the development of
AIDS as a dread new disease. How can one not be excited
and continually refreshed [Marden].

I Tap into My Own Newness

Some professors keep their enthusiasm for what appear to be quite
personal reasons, reasons that defy categorization:

I am often asked how I remain so enthusiastic in my teaching. I think fear of failure plays a great role. I worry a lot
about being boring or irrelevant. Perhaps my training as a
competitive athlete has helped me "get up" for a class. I
pace, I go to the bathroom a lot, I get worked up before a
class. Never have I walked into a class without being a little
frightened. Bored? No. Scared? Yes. As provost at Tufts, I
have every reason to walk away from my classes, every
excuse. But I cannot. I am teaching even more than ever,
because I need it [Gittleman].

I try alone or with students to create some spectacle, some
mutual project or challenge or event, which in a creative
and at times outrageous way serves to embody our learning
and be fun. Sometimes it is an evening at my home, to
which my students must bring something relevant to our
work together in class (a poem, costume, appropriate food,
and so on). Sometimes it is a literature "lab," in which we
learn the metrics of nursery rhymes. Sometimes it is a theater
event. Sometimes it is a party, in which we perform a non-
stop reading of *Ulysses* (twenty-eight hours and four minutes). Our college is structured on the 4-1-4 calendar, so that
January term allows wonderfully creative (even internation-
ally located), project-centered courses—a continuing lure
away from the dull demons of boredom. As I write all this,

however, it becomes clear to me that much of my not being bored is in my own mindset, combined with the choice I have made to teach in a setting where small classes are the norm. I love rereading the masterworks of literature; but just as much, I enjoy the experience of students learning how to read well, how to draw conclusions about what they are reading, how to appreciate the nuances of image and tone, how to be moved—authentically and irretrievably. Every semester I learn from them something new about the literature I teach and about the ways to teach and learn. So I guess the experience of teaching itself keeps me interested [Empric].

I have been blessed with a very bad memory. It is an embarrassment when a colleague asks, "Now who was the author of that famous monograph on Donne's 'Valediction'?" But when the sixth student in as many years comments on the Edenic imagery in *The Awakening*, my bad memory makes it easy for me to exclaim, "Hey, I never thought of that before!" It may not be true, but it certainly seems true at the time. I reread each poem, short story, or novel before teaching it again and almost always discover what feels like a new idea. As a consequence, it is easy for me to bring to class discussions something of the enthusiasm that comes naturally in an early reading of a work. However, after a while, even a bad memory cannot prevent *The Scarlet Letter*, taught for the twentieth time, from being familiar. Then I try to remember what it was like when I first knew it. If I cannot muster genuine enthusiasm, I fake it—without apology. A good teacher has to be a good actor, too. I discover that when I try to act out the excitement I recall from early readings, I usually begin actually to feel it. Besides, each time I teach a work, with any luck I am a different person than on the last go-round. So my final tactic for revitalization is to tap into my own newness, connecting the old worlds with what I have learned and with the person I have become since my last reading [Carson].

There are many techniques, many tricks of the trade, to keep professors stimulated and stimulating. We can scramble for new courses and new sabbaticals. We can get caught up in learning more and more about the subjects we teach. We can publish. We can force ourselves to recall that because our students are different each year, so are our courses. But perhaps most of all, we need to develop a habit of mind, a way of looking at ourselves and the work we do, that will serve as a continuing reminder that nothing involving human beings is ever quite the same. Perhaps, in the end, the best trick that the best professors have found is the discovery that with all the scholarship and learning and human contact good teaching entails, our profession packs along its own perpetual antidote to boredom.

*Experts love to give advice, and expert professors are no
exception. When asked what advice they would give to novices
in our profession, they are happy to say something pithy,
useful, and idealistic about how to teach.*

"Erase the Board and Turn Off the Light": Advice to Novices about Teaching

Teaching is the art and craft of dealing with people. When we professors are asked for advice about teaching, we tend to think most often about "people words" like honesty, integrity, openness, commitment, humaneness, faith, and caring. Not one of us CASE professors, however, mentioned the need to have a sense of humor. That is funny, isn't it?

Teaching Backwards

Actually, almost no one ever asks me for advice about teaching. When someone does, I rarely give it, and I generally resent people who try to tell me how to teach. They can never know the circumstances under which I teach. They do not know how little I may know about my subject. They do not know what particular mix of students I have in a given class. Most important, they do not know much about my personal style. What works for them works for them. It will probably not work for me. For that reason, I refrain from giving advice about teaching. When pressed, however, I sometimes say that while I do not give advice, I can try to explain a little about how I teach. I usually say that I teach backwards. In fact, most

P. G. Beidler (ed.). *Distinguished Teachers on Effective Teaching.*
New Directions for Teaching and Learning, no. 28. San Francisco: Jossey-Bass, Winter 1986.

of the courses I have described in earlier chapters are examples of what I call teaching backwards. All I mean by this phrase is that whenever I can, I try following precisely the opposite of someone else's advice, try teaching just the opposite of whatever is considered the standard way.

We all know, for example, that teachers are supposed to teach subjects in which they are trained experts. In my first course on American Indians, however, I taught a subject in which I had no training and emphatically was not an expert. That was doing it all backwards, but what an exhilarating experience it was to be openly and unashamedly learning alongside my students.

We all know that teachers are supposed to dispense information. I have discovered that I teach better, however, not when I am giving out information but when I dig for information by asking questions.

We all know that teachers are supposed to give exams after they have presented and discussed the material to be covered by the exam. I have found, however, that I teach American literature best if I ask the questions—and demand that the students answer them in writing and for credit—before I have discussed my views on the literature assigned for a given class period. That is all backwards, but my students learn to learn on their own that way, not merely from me.

We all know that freshman English students need a textbook to learn from, but one semester I had my freshmen write their own textbook, drawing from what they knew, but could not easily express, about what makes one piece of writing better than another. That was doing it backwards, but in learning how to find the words for what they intuitively knew, they learned better how to write than if I had forced them to read someone else's textbook on writing.

We all know that the college classroom is a sheltered, indoor place where students learn theories they can later apply to real life. For the most part, however, I skip the theories and teach inductively. I present cases or poems or stories or novels. I insist that my students read them carefully on their own. I encourage them, if they are of a mind to, to make generalizations from the different cases, poems, stories, or novels. The theories are their business to deduce, not mine to lay out. My job is to make them read *Walden* and to show them how to put a new roof on an old house. I do it all backwards, but my students learn more about theories of self-reliance and why self-reliance is a central theme in American life than if I tell them the theories and let them find the cases on their own once they leave my ivory tower.

I do not advise that others teach backwards, or at least not backwards in the same way that I do. If I were to give a single piece of advice about teaching, however, it would be to challenge every piece of advice anyone gives about how to teach, to try doing just the opposite, just to see what happens. My advice, then, is to do exactly the opposite of what the other CASE finalists have said to do in response to this question:

If you could pass on to a beginning college teacher just one piece of advice about how to teach, what would it be?

There was great variety in the advice given. What we have here, then, is an "alphabet soup" of advice about teaching.

They Deserve No Less

The most consistent piece of advice given was to center teaching on the student. Even here, however, no two professors put the advice in quite the same way:

> *Remember your audience.* Young teachers are apt to be so ill at ease that they internalize what they have to say, ignoring the process of communication and even blocking out the listeners. Most lectures can lose some students, so I put an outline on the board and point to it now and then to show where I am in the text. And I watch the audience to see how they are receiving things. I try to involve the audience, to get them to ask questions. I tell a story about some class member who has done an interesting thing. Last week, it was the story of Humphrey the Whale, the beleaguered cetacean who lost his way and swam up a river. I was able to discuss the real-life drama with a couple of my students, who had been in the armada trying to steer him away from San Francisco Bay. I lighten my heavy text now and then with short anecdotes that show that scientists are people. Last week, I told about the time I spent two weeks sitting in a giant tree overhanging the Amazon River listening to the *boutu rosada,* or Amazon River dolphin, as it swam in a muddy eddy beneath me. I told about the stinging ants and fern patches I had to step over on my way up the sloping trunk, and I imitated the ululating voice of the dolphin as it scanned the murk with swings of its head [Norris].

> *Be humane.* Remember that each new student has many apprehensions and responsibilities about which you know nothing. Be stern. Be congratulatory. Be encouraging. Be an example. In appearance, in oral presentations, in writing, in scientific techniques, set the standard. Give students a role model [Richason].

> *Know your students.* Knowing your field is not enough. Not only will knowing your students enable you to communicate better with them, it will provide the inspiration you will

need to do the best job you can do. And as you come to know your students, you will realize that you must do the best job you can do. They deserve no less [Hofman].

Remember that your subject has meaning and value for the human race. If your students are hostile to your subject, that is probably because they were taught it badly in high school, were frightened of it because of its terminology and unfamiliar apparatus, or heard it disparaged as "sissy stuff" by their parents or friends. In any case, the thing is to present it as enchantingly and interestingly as possible, without reference to any of their hostility. Refer to your subject always as if it were irresistible and full of gaiety. Soon your students will find it so [Vendler].

Respect your students. Being a department head, I occasionally get complaints from students about the conduct of some of the faculty. What surprises me most is that some faculty have so little respect for the students they teach [Bass].

A Seeing-Eye Parrot?

One way of showing respect for one's students, of course, is to be honest with them, even if it means demonstrating one's own life, feelings, and limitations:

Be honest. Being a model of intellectual and personal honesty will save you from the expectation that you need to know everything and will save students from shirking the responsibility of their own learning. Honestly commit yourself to the profession. Honestly evaluate your commitment from time to time. Honestly admit mistakes, or that you do not know, or that you are new, or that this course is on its maiden voyage. Honestly share your ideas on pedagogy, your reasons for certain assignments, your hypotheses, plans, goals. Evaluate others and yourself as honestly as you can, given the evidence you have honestly worked to collect. Then be forgiving of mistakes (including your own) and rest in Chaucer's assurance that the intention is all. One more word: Do it all with tact [Empric].

Show your students that you care deeply—both about what you are teaching and about them. If they can see that you love your subject, they are likely to be caught up by that affection, envy it, and want to experience it themselves. If they are convinced that you like and respect them, that you regard them as partners in learning rather than receptacles for your wisdom, they will forgive you many mistakes. They will be willing to take risks with you, and they may help you discover things about your field—and yourself—that you never imagined [Carson].

Be yourself. Everyone has a "real" personality under the everyday veneer we all wear for protection. The closer your students can come to the real you, and the better they can see who you are and why you want to be there, the more they will join you. Be open and honest. Make fair rules and stick to them [Clark].

Bring yourself into the classroom. You should be human, interested in students, and willing to poke fun at number one. Convince your students that you believe in what you are teaching, in them, and in yourself. To do this, you need to know a lot about yourself, and you need to let students know some of it. As an absent-minded blind professor, I sometimes get lost on my way from home to the campus. One day this fall, I told my students about being lost among the swings, slides, and teeter-totters of an elementary school playground. For the balance of the lecture, we examined the economics of owning a seeing-eye dog, taking a taxi to campus, and the likely success of a seeing-eye-parrot venture [Sisler].

Be absolutely honest. Be knowledgeable. Be passionate. Love what you are doing [Saltman].

Communicate your love of your subject. It is important to show students how a subject is personalized in the teacher. A beginning teacher should not fear taking a risk to expose that personal dimension of the subject. In graduate school, I studied under a man who was considered by many to be the world authority on Descartes. I learned a great deal from him, and his classes were extraordinarily stimulating. I wrote one of my papers for him on Cartesian proofs for the existence of God. I really wrestled with those proofs and had considerable difficulty assessing some aspects of them. When the world authority returned my papers, we talked a bit about my work, and then I asked him the big question:

"What do *you* think of the proofs?" He looked at me and smiled and said, "I don't think that I have yet plumbed their depths." That was the end of the conversation, and I felt greatly cheated. A scholar of his magnitude surely had more to say than that, but he never gave me an opportunity to learn what he personally thought. Instead, I learned something else: that I have a responsibility to my students to show how I form opinions and to risk exposing my tentative hypotheses. A teacher should not be afraid to do that. It is largely a matter of trust, both in ourselves and in our students. It is also a matter of commitment to the enterprise of learning, which has never progressed without individuals taking such risks [Ulrich].

Be yourself and master of your subject [Ratliff].

Reveal your fallabilities. Show that you are human. You are, after all. As young Ph.D.s, we often feel like experts, ready to hang out a shingle and practice the art of teaching. Perhaps in the aftermath of receiving our advanced degrees, we feel a bit infallible. But pride goes before a fall. Twenty-odd years ago, when I first came to Colgate, I remember going through considerable trouble to set up a flawless demonstration experiment to show how Galileo deduced the law of falling bodies. I filled a four-foot glass cylinder with water, intending to drop a lead ball inside that cylinder, as well as one outside it (in the air), so that students could simultaneously compare the relative speeds at which the balls fell in the media of water and air. I rehearsed the experiment several times to make sure I could do it just right. Then, when I did it in class, the lead ball on the outside hit the base of the cylinder and the entire apparatus toppled over like a falling redwood, shattering the glass and splashing everyone in the classroom with the two or three gallons of water. I was embarrassed but then laughed at the whole experience, and at least for a moment the students knew I was not the infallible professor [Aveni].

The Ground Is Always Shifting

Aside from the two large pieces of advice—showing concern for students and being utterly honest and open in dealings with them—there was little unanimity in the responses:

Be flexible. Do not pay attention to someone who has only one piece of advice about how to teach. It is both a curse and a blessing of teaching that there is no one way. Teaching continues to delight me because the ground is always shifting under my feet. What worked today may not work tomorrow. In addition to being flexible, be generous [Eble].

Keep learning. Remember that teaching is a full-time job—twelve months a year, even if you get paid only for nine. Use your time wisely and well, but use it fully. You are not just a teacher. You are also still a learner. You can bluff your departmental chairperson and your colleagues when you cut corners, and deans are really easy. But there are two people you cannot deceive if you have not both prepared fully and continually renewed your knowledge—a nineteen-year-old college student and yourself [Marden].

Move about the classroom. It is hard for me to see how anyone can stand still and be interesting. Being still is a way to a knowledge of God, but I do not believe it is an effective way to teach literature to other mortals. Remember: To worship, be still; to teach, move [Higgs].

Be scared. Be a worrier. Be afraid of failure. Then translate these feelings into energy, careful preparation, and ambition [Gittleman].

Believe. Have faith in the greatness of teaching as a vocation. Have faith in your students. Have faith in yourself. Bishop Tutu said that no Christian can be anything but an optimist. He would not mind, I think, if I said that of the teacher [Eichner].

Erase the board and turn off the light. That is the only counsel given me by the dean when I first came to the university. I would like to tell a beginner some stories about successes and failures, unexpected brilliance, growth, and character development on the part of students. I would like to share some anecdotes about great colleagues: personal courage on the part of one, whose wife became his eyes when he went blind and continued to teach; the absolute candor of another, who knew it was time to stop teaching before the evaluations reflected it. Consider the appropriateness of the remark of Holden Caulfield: "First you are good, then you know you are good, then you are no good." But the exciting thing about seeing beginning college teachers is knowing that they will experience their own anecdotes. Anyway, there are two reasons for erasing the board. One is to give your successor a clean slate. The other is to celebrate the dictum of Meister Eckhart, who said that "only the hand that knows how to erase can write the true thing." As for turning off the light, I started teaching when turning off the light was evidence of sensitivity to the environment, to natural resources, to frugality as a feature of the learning enterprise. It assumes, as well, that during your hour with students the light was on, even when a tolerance for ambiguity or complexity of thought or the dark side of things was being probed. Let me see. What was the question [Albertson]?

The question was . . . . Like most absent-minded professors, I have a rotten memory. There are three things I can never remember. I can never remember a face. I can never remember a name. And I can never remember . . . I forget what the third thing was.

Professors love what they do for a living because it provides them freedom, variety, a chance to keep on learning, and the opportunity both to be near young people and, through them, to change the world. They cannot imagine a better life.

"Why Don't You Get a Real Job?": Professors Who Enjoy Their Work

Teaching is not an easy life, at least not if it is done with seriousness, conscience, energy, humor, and compassion. It is, however, an intensely satisfying profession for those who do it well. Over and over again, professors say, "I cannot imagine a better way to spend my life." For some, the biggest wonder of it all is that someone actually pays them to do this thing they love.

I Teach Because of Lisa

Halfway through last semester, Lisa made an appointment to see me. She said she wanted to talk about the paper on Poe's "Ligeia" I had returned to her the period before with an A- and a lengthy written comment. In the comment, I told her that she had a soft thesis, a weak organizational pattern, and a cowardly conclusion. I had been hoping Lisa would come in sometime, because she always looked so angry in class. She never talked in class, but she had an expressive face, a face that did not lie, a face that said louder than words, "I am unhappy here." We made an appointment for the following afternoon, when I had a couple of hours free.

P. G. Beidler (ed.). *Distinguished Teachers on Effective Teaching.*
New Directions for Teaching and Learning, no. 28. San Francisco: Jossey-Bass, Winter 1986.

"I don't agree with the grade you gave me on this paper," Lisa said, for an opener. She waited for me to respond. I played a hunch, figuring Lisa was different from most students who came in to complain about a grade, and asked her if she thought it was too high. She looked startled. "Yes. That was a dumb paper, and it didn't go anywhere. You shouldn't have given it an A. Also, I found your comment surprisingly tactless."

I replied that although her paper was one of the better papers I had received, still there was lots of room for improvement in her writing. I had used the high grade to reflect my appreciation of her understanding of the story and her graceful way with words. The tactless part of my comment, I said, was designed to help her see that her paper was flawed and could have been stronger. Then I asked Lisa why it was important to her to put me on the defensive like that.

She did not answer my question. Instead, she countered with, "Why are you at Lehigh? You don't fit the pattern here."

I explained that even though Lehigh was known mostly for its engineering curriculum, we have a strong English department, and I like my colleagues. I explained that I like teaching writing and literature in what sometimes seems like an alien environment. I said I get a kick out of introducing literature to people who think they hate it. I explained that many of our finest English majors started as engineering majors but decided they did not like engineering. They excelled in English, I said, because they had strong mathematics and analytical skill, and they could think clearly. I explained that it is fun working with people like that. I explained that I like living near a stream not far from the Delaware River, in the rural valley where I spent some of my very youthful years. And I explained that Lehigh had offered me a job, which was more than thousands of other colleges and universities around the world had done. Why, I asked, had she asked?

"Because I hate this place. I came here to be an engineer, because I was good in math and wanted to make a lot of money. Now I'm stuck here. I can't get this kind of financial aid anywhere else because my freshman grades are so bad, and I would lose too many of my credits if I tried to transfer to a real university. I feel like a jewel in a dungheap. And that's what you are, too. You know that, don't you? My God, you act like you enjoy teaching in this place. Neither one of us belongs here."

I said that it was a good thing we had found each other, then.

We talked on and on. Shortly before we parted that afternoon, I told Lisa that I thought she was making excuses, blaming Lehigh for her unhappiness. It was not Lehigh's job to make her happy. That was her job. I suggested that she stop moaning about the dungheap of her surroundings and start polishing the jewel. I told her it upset me to see her make generalizations about five thousand people, most of whom she never met. I suggested that if she scratched around, she might find some more jewels, and in doing so discover that the dungheap, or least a corner of it, was really a jewel heap. "Why," I asked her, "don't you accept some responsibility for your surroundings and stop using them as excuses?"

Lisa wept. I gave her a tissue. We talked some more. Then I told her I had to leave for a meeting, but I hoped she would stop in to see me again. She did not need to have an excuse like complaining about a grade. She could just come in to continue our chat. She said she would like to. We made an appointment for the following week.

We had many more talks before the end of the semester. We even wrote notes to each other. Lisa told me about her family. She introduced me to her boyfriend ("another one of the jewels at Lehigh"). A month later she told me—with dancing eyes, because she knew I would be excited—that she had decided to be a writer. I said that was a wonderful ambition, but cautioned that it could mean a lonely life.

Lisa told me that she wanted to write her own weekly column in the *Brown and White*, Lehigh's student newpaper, but knew that they would not let her because she was not on the regular journalism staff and did not want to be on it. I suggested that she draft a couple of sample columns and send them with a cover letter to the new editor. She did. I was pleased, of course, because Lisa showed me the samples. I could see that she was starting to buy into this place, was trying to scratch around in the dungheap and help it to become a garden of jewels.

Lisa did not get her column. The editor said he was going to have to shorten the paper because of his limited budget and devote even a bigger percentage of the paper to advertising so that he could pay off some debts from earlier semesters. I told Lisa that I was disappointed. She asked me if she could do an independent study with me, a creative writing course in which she would write some short stories. I said, "Sure, if you will consider sending your best story to *Redbook* or some other magazine." She said that *Redbook* was just a dumb women's magazine. I smiled and told her I doubted that she was good enough to get published in a dumb women's magazine like that. She smiled and said she would show me.

Teaching is the right profession for me because of Lisa. It is good for me to spend time in the presence of Lisa. We smile. We talk about why some writers have to live near a body of water. (Lisa says it is because they can write more from the "source" that way.) We consider whether Queequeg's being illiterate is a serious limitation. (Lisa decides that it is, because mere goodness is not enough to influence so literate a man as Ahab.) Lisa laughs when I tell her that I do almost all my Christmas shopping in a hardware store. When I discover that she has never heard of Robert Pirsig's *Zen and the Art of Motorcycle Maintenance*, I give her a copy, explaining that although I did not buy it in a hardware store, she will be wrenched by it.

There is only one Lisa, but she proved to me that her name is legion for those of us lucky enough to be in this profession. Lisa is my answer when I ask myself why I have chosen and why I remain in this profession. My question to my fellow CASE workers was this:

Why is teaching the right profession for you? It is, isn't it?

The answer the CASE finalists gave to the second part of the question was a resounding "Yes!" Of course this is the right profession. Is there a better one? We hear a lot about decreasing job satisfaction and morale in the profession of teaching. We hear that the rift between faculty and administration is widening, that the best minds no longer enter this profession, that the pressures to publish have made too many of us perish, that instead of tenure many good teachers get manure, that there is more prestige in almost any other profession than this, that we are shamefully underpaid, that our students are coming to us less and less literate and more and more interested merely in having us prepare them for high-paying secure jobs. And more. Still, these professors love what they do and love most of those they do it with. They do not wish they were doing something else.

A Pervert and a Masochist

CASE professors like associating with students. Of course, there are some students who make professors happy to see the end of the semester, but by and large we like associating with young people and with students of any age who are on the brink of discovery:

> Usually this question gets asked in a different way: It is homecoming. The foliage is spectacular. The football team won the big game. All is right with the college and the world. The young alumna tells me about what is happening in her life—the new job, the great opportunity, the books she has read, the interesting relationship she is handling well, the ideas she has. Then, in the spirit of true kindness, she thanks me for my efforts on her behalf and asks the question: "Why don't you get a real job?" The answer, of course, is standing straight and tall right in front of me. I can think of no more honorable way to waste my time than in contributing to the opportunities of youth [Marden].

> Teaching was the right profession for me because I was better at conveying ideas than any other thing I could do. After twenty-six years if it, teaching is still the best profession for me because it keeps me in touch with the most exciting people in the world: college freshmen and juniors [Sisler].

I like chemistry. I like doing the experimentation by which the concepts of chemistry are acquired. I like doing the mental exercises by which the concepts of chemistry are formulated. I like chemistry because it is the vehicle that enables me to interact with young people in a purposeful way [Hofman].

I love college life. I love being near a gymnasium and being able to work out with the varsity baseball team. I love being able to order books for the library and then being the first person to read them. I love being with young people who are the same age I was thirty years ago, when John Schabacker first got hold of me. I love making lights go on in people's heads [Gittleman].

Teaching is the only profession I have ever tried. I have been twenty-two years at it, and I love it. I enjoy getting up in the morning and I cannot wait to get to class. I enjoy the kids and enjoy helping them develop in the formative years, when they so much need guidance to help them to be on their own. Those who have graduated and returned to visit me often make me realize they needed me. Being needed is important [Aveni].

As an adult scholar, I am a centered, open person who loves a good joke, and I am a good and imaginative naturalist with something to say about where we came from, who we are, and what is happening to our world. I have also learned that there is nothing more personally rewarding than service to young people. Put all that together, and what else could I be [Norris]?

Teaching is my passion. If it were not the right profession for me, I would be a pervert and a masochist. I am neither. I have been teaching for thirty-two years. It gives me tremendous pleasure to do what I am doing. I love the university. I cannot imagine a more wonderful, exciting, and enriching environment. When I see students come back to say how much their interaction with this university, and in part with me, has meant in their lives, that is a reward very few others can share. And deep down inside, if you really want to know, I think that the university is a fountain of youth. Every year I begin anew. I am surrounded by young, vital, and inquiring minds. I try to keep up with my students. It is an exciting challenge [Saltman].

A Voyeur and a Peeping Tom

We professors stay in teaching partly because it affords us an opportunity, without having to apologize or pay tuition, to continue our education.

Teaching is the right profession for me because it gives me the opportunity both to revitalize the knowledge I have already acquired and to gain new knowledge in other disciplines. In my time as a professor of philosophy, I have also taken courses in the departments of biology, chemistry, and religious studies. I have just completed a third master's degree, this one in counseling. All of this allows me to make extraordinary and exciting interconnections. I cannot imagine a life-style that is more challenging, exciting, and rewarding. It is hard for me to imagine myself doing anything else [Ulrich].

College teaching provides me with the freedom to pursue a variety of interests. It allows me not only to share what I know but also to grow intellectually. I cannot imagine a life without that growing and that sharing [Richason].

I did not realize, until I was on active duty in the Korean War and had an intense urge to go back to school, that this was the profession I should be in. I can remember trying to analyze this feeling while on long marches and realizing that I wanted to better understand why birds fly south in the winter. That fall—and the following fall, when I had the same feeling—I decided that if things worked out, I would return to college and stay in an academic setting. Although there are many other things I would like to do, none would satisfy me as much as teaching and learning [Bass].

I have many professions within teaching. I am an explainer. I am a writer. I am a scientist who likes problems and puzzles, of which literature and language offer a fine array. Teaching is part psychology, part theater, part counseling, part communication. I like all these professions. Most of all, I like the constant self-education that teaching provokes. Preparing a new course involves giving oneself a self-seminar in the subject first. It is disturbing and tiring, but finally helpful and pleasurable [Vendler].

My wife says that I belong on the campus because I am a slow learner. It has taken me a lifetime to get a college education. It is really because I cannot remember everything and have to keep going back over it. Seriously, I have to learn. Learning is my daily bread. It is wholly selfish, I fear, but I feel more alive in a community of learners than anywhere else. I am a voyeur, a peeping tom. I like to watch other people doing it almost as much as doing it myself. But unexpected (yet dependable) flashes of intuition or dogged discoveries or familiar ideas enlighten and warm me and make my joy complete. Every day. But I must mention also one special pleasure of the profession: friends we would give anything to cultivate if we were not on the campus, friends we take for granted year after year and discover anew each time an occasion makes dialogue possible [Albertson].

A Relay into the Future

We college professors like teaching because we feel that it gives us an opportunity to shape the world around us, the world that will be after us:

College teaching is the right profession for me because I like to explain things, and there is no other group with whom I would rather work than college students. Their lives are ahead of them. During these four years, girls become women and boys become men. Through these men and women, I may make some small contribution toward achieving a better world, a world in which all persons live in dignity. These men and women are destined to make decisions that determine whether basic human needs are met, whether unjust social and economic inequalities are removed, and whether people are in control of their own destinies. The serious global problems of poverty, environmental pollution, and nuclear proliferation need to be tackled by broad-gauged persons who have well-trained minds and who are firmly committed to a set of moral values, persons who think in terms of the solidarity of humankind. Among my students are some really good prospects for tackling these problems. I am privileged to be associated with them [Ratliff].

One of our certainties is that we are only passing by. I am grateful that while passing by I have touched other lives, that I have been able to share what I know and think, that I have been able to listen to my students, encourage them to write well, be artists with the spoken and the written word. An autobiographical note of Louise Bogan speaks for me:

"In a time lacking in truth and certainty, filled with anguish and despair, no woman should be shamefaced in attempting to give back to the world, through her work, a portion of its heart" [Eichner].

Teaching provides the opportunity to share what I know, to give something of myself, and to help influence the future in ways that I hope will be beneficial. In my view, no other profession carries the kind of responsibility that ours does for integrity, social service, and ethical development [Clark].

Teaching is right for me because I love people almost as much as I love ideas, and I can think of no other occupation in which I can live with both nearly all the time. I gain immense satisfaction from understanding complex issues, from experiencing intriguing patterns, and from problem solving. But the pleasure is heightened by the opportunity to pass on my perceptions, to feel myself part of a relay into the future [Empric].

And They Pay Me for This!

Over and over, CASE finalists express the pure joy of teaching. They are still a little surprised that they actually draw paychecks for leading the life that others might consider paying to have the privilege of leading:

When I was young, I harbored a dream of becoming an Aimée Semple McPherson kind of evangelist. I think what I wanted as much as redeemed souls was the sense that I was the one who had redeemed them. Although I have lost the faith that engendered that dream, I think I have kept the evangelism. I want to make a difference in people's lives. I believe that in teaching, I do that. I teach, too, because it makes me feel good. I love seeing students moved by the literature we are discussing. I love what I can see in students' eyes when they say, "Oh. *Oh,* yeah!" I love to see students get so excited about ideas that they can hardly contain themselves. I love being able to say honestly that they have taught me something. I love the sense of perennial youthfulness that goes with constantly exchanging the role of teacher for that of student. Teaching is right for me because it offers the perfect way to combine my downright self-indulgence with a hope for self-transcendence [Carson].

My earliest and highest aspiration was to be a writer. I turned to college teaching because I guessed that I might have a better chance of earning a living by doing it than writing. Much later, after much writing and teaching, I found out that I had chosen rightly, but for the wrong reason. I realized I could not have pursued the solitariness necessary to being the kind of writer I aspired to be. I realized that some strong part of me needed the interchange with other people over things we were interested in. That living contact with other human beings at the point of learning something was the fundamental necessity. Communing in books and art and music and drama was also necessary, but because it required me to be by myself for long periods of time, it was not the prime necessity. I have been immensely happy with my work because it has enabled me to go back and forth between being private and being public. I have been paid for doing so, and I still accept with some wonder that such a favorable combination of circumstances should fall upon me [Eble].

Teaching is exactly the right profession for me because I like to read, I like to share ideas, and I like to imagine. Teaching is in some ways a racket, because, as Leslie Fiedler says, they pay you to read. I also enjoy being around young people, and I like to laugh a lot. For some reason, the classrooom is the funniest place I know of. I love to hear gales of laughter coming out of a classroom. Then I know something important is going on. I am at my worst in the classrooom when I take myself and the material too seriously. Randall Jarrell said he would pay to teach. I cannot afford to do that, but I understand what he meant [Higgs].

All is not warmth and violets in this profession of ours, but we professors tend to love what we do. And why would we not love it? There was a day, after all, when we paid tuition to do what we now get paid for doing: associating with fine professors, having ready access to a library or a laboratory, being surrounded by mostly pleasant young people, being forced to learn new things all the time, being encouraged to write, having an identification card that lets us into college sports events. Add to all that the satisfaction of knowing that we have the power to touch, the power to matter in people's lives and to influence through them the shape of the future.
How could we not love what we do?

Index

A

Albertson, R. G., 5; advice on teaching from, 81-82; on boredom, 69-70; on goal for students, 45; on publishing, 36; on teaching profession, 88-89; on writing, 58
Alice in Wonderland, 58
Aristotle, 57
Aveni, A. F., 5; advice on teaching from, 80; on boredom, 70; on chosen profession, 87; on goal for students, 46-47; on learning by doing, 54-55; on research, 33; on teaching and real world, 22
Awakening, The, 73

B

Bailey, J., 66
Barton, T. F., 12-13
Bass, W. M., III, 5-6; advice on teaching from, 78; on goal for students, 46; on learning by doing, 55; on lecturing, 69; on research, 32; on teaching and real world, 22; on teaching profession, 88;
Bates College, 10-11
Beidler, P. G., 2
Berwanger, G., 14-15
Bogan, L., 89-90
Bonner, J., 13
Booth, W., 3-4
Boredom: avoiding, 63-65, 73-74; change to avoid, 69-70; and enthusiasm, 70-73; professional absence of, 67-68; students as antidote to, 65-67

C

California, University of: at San Diego, 13; at Santa Cruz, 11
Carroll College, 12
Carson, B. H., 6; advice on teaching from, 78-79; on boredom, 73; on diversity of learning styles, 59; on goal for students, 46; on joy of teaching, 90; on research and publishing, 39-40; on teaching and real world, 20-21
Caulfield, H., 81
Chaucer, 7, 17, 26, 30, 44, 78
Clark, M. E., 6-7; advice on teaching from, 79; on goal for students, 47; on learning by doing, 55; on liberal arts, 25; on research, 37-38; on student enthusiasm, 66-67; on teaching profession, 90;
Colgate University, 5
Confidence, 44-45
Cooke, P., 66
Cornell University, 13
Council for Advancement and Support of Education (CASE), 1
Cowles, R., 11-12

D

Daly, R. W., 9
Davidson College, 12
Dayton, University of, 14
"Death of Ivan Illyich, The," 60
Descartes, 79-80

E

Earlham College, 3
East Tennesse State University, 9
Eble, K. E., 7, 44; advice on teaching from, 80-81; on boredom, 70; on how students learn, 57; on research and publishing, 38-39; on teaching and real world, 20; on teaching profession, 91
Eckerd College, 8
Eckhart, M., 82
Edwards, J., 66
Eichner, M., 7; advice on teaching from, 81; on boredom, 68; on goal for students, 48; on learning by example, 59; on liberal arts, 25; on